NEW ORLEANS
STYLE

ANDI EATON

Foreword by Stephanie Granada

THE
History
PRESS

Andi Eaton

10·1·14

Published by The History Press
Charleston, SC 29403
www.historypress.net

Copyright © 2014 by Andi Eaton
All rights reserved

Back cover, left: Photo by Kaela Rodehorst Williams.

First published 2014

Manufactured in the United States

ISBN 978.1.62619.641.4

Library of Congress CIP data applied for.

For my grandparents, Norma Louise Tebeau and Shirley and William Van Dresser.

CONTENTS

FOREWORD

It doesn't take long for someone to fall in love with New Orleans. The Victorian architecture, the rich Creole history and the zealous locals all come together to create a spirit that stays with you long after you leave. In no area is that reflected better than in the city's style. This has always been the case—after all, this is where the seersucker suit, now a staple of a southern gent's wardrobe and, in its more feminine tailoring, a southern woman's too, was born in the 1900s thanks to Joseph Haspel, whose brand, much like the rest of the city, is in a state of revival. For further proof of NOLA's timeless style factor, just look at images of a rumpled yet elegant Truman Capote walking the streets of his hometown in suit pants with cuffs rolled up, Kitty Carlisle sparkling in pearls and gold gowns well into her nineties or the impossible intricacy of a 1940s Mardi Gras Indian headdress.

Although rooted in the same traditions that make the South distinct, New Orleans style is notably looser, more colorful and deeply personal. The city was recently described to me as an extension of the Caribbean rather than a southern city, and the vibrantly hued, gauzy nature of the residents' wardrobes vividly displays this. Although New Orleans has never lacked in style, it was not until the last couple years that the fashion culture, previously overshadowed by the city's food and music, took center stage. What is happening now is a continuation of the chic absurd mixed with classic authenticity that has always made the city beautiful. Fashion insiders around the country are taking notice now more than ever due in large part to a tribe of young entrepreneurs who choose to call NOLA home, such as Sarah Elizabeth Dewey and Jolie Bensen of Jolie & Elizabeth, who refreshed the seersucker dress; the humble yet dynamic Lisa Iacono, who revived the city's textile industry with her factory NOLA Sewn, where she and her crew are responsible for manufacturing pieces for more than thirty American-made brands; Stirling Barrett of Krewe du Optic, an artist who reconfigured his skills to carefully craft what's set to be the next great sunglass company—each pair promoting the city's heritage with names that take after streets around town; and, of course, Andi Eaton, a powerhouse of a woman who always looks perfectly at ease despite the fact that behind the scenes she's running a blog, a boutique, a clothing brand and the city's twice-annual Fashion Week, a feat made possible and successful due to her genuine love for the city and a drive to keep it moving forward.

When I first met Andi, standing out with green mermaid hair and even brighter threads, I thought she perfectly epitomized that mix of elegant, quirky, feminine and edgy that makes the city unique. We met to discuss Fashion Week, an event that I'd heard of and had admittedly pushed aside, having been oversaturated by the influx of fashion weeks that have popped up over the last five years. But I quickly found this event was nothing to snuff at. With its unique slant of promoting regional brands and authenticity, many say it was a catalyst for the rejuvenation of the city's fashion industry. This is why I cannot imagine a person better suited to pen this book. As the city continues to move toward the forefront of our country's style culture, Andi will no doubt continue to shape and represent the new face of New Orleans.

STEPHANIE GRANADA
Style Editor at *Southern Living*

PREFACE

Through pestilence, hurricanes, and conflagrations the people continued to sing. They sang through the long oppressive years of conquering the swampland and fortifying the town against the ever threatening Mississippi. They are singing today. An irrepressible joie de vivre maintains the unbroken thread of music through the air.
—Lura Robinson, It's An Old New Orleans Custom, *1948*

Not so many years ago, if you had asked a typical person on the street of an average American city to describe New Orleans, the picture would likely go something like this: "Beads and bare bodies!" "Throw me something, mister!" "Hurricanes and hand grenades" and "Wild nights on Bourbon Street!" Or perhaps, the vision would be on the opposite end of the spectrum.

Perhaps the vision would be of Hurricane Katrina, certainly the most memorable storm of the last decades and one that local people set time by—"pre-Katrina" versus "post-Katrina." And while for quite some time much of the world's knowledge of the city, built on three hundred years of blended French, Spanish, African and Caribbean influence, may have been overshadowed by the

> We dance even
> if there's no radio. We
> drink at funerals. We talk
> too much and laugh too
> loud and live too large and,
> frankly, we're suspicious of
> others who don't.
> —Chris Rose

story of the party or that natural disaster, New Orleanians have always known their city holds a much deeper magic.

Spend a little time with the locals and there's a totally different tale to be told. New Orleans is a city founded on music: "Ask a little kid what he wants to be and instead of saying 'I want to be a policeman,' or 'I want to be a fireman,' he says, 'I want to be a musician.'"[1] It's home to festivities and food, architecture and design and artists of all genres. There's those who play and show their work in high-end concert halls and galleries and those who are "street entrepreneurs." It's a city where artists survive and thrive as an integral part of the community. It has a style uniquely its own, influenced by the sounds, sights, tastes and traditions of the people who built it.

It is a city whose icons have led entire movements—jazz music, civil rights, Mardi Gras—and inspired fashions copied by the rest of the world, including festival fashion, flappers, seersucker and tropical style. From the regal and exuberant style of the French to the Spanish sartorial influence to the pride of the Creole and Cajun people, New Orleanians embody their history and their future every day in the clothes they wear.

The people of New Orleans have complete confidence in who they are and have an unshakable dedication to maintaining that identity. This story will take a look at the city's founders from the early explorers to the King's Daughters and Bellocq's Storyville brothel girls to the Carnival Queens and Kings in their trimmings, as well as the elegance of the jazz musicians both past and present. Discover here the heritage behind the city's most notable and notorious and take a look neighborhood by neighborhood at the style of the city.

ACKNOWLEDGEMENTS

Muchas gracias to my dear friend Luca DiMartino for giving me the opportunity to live in his family's home in Spain while writing this book and for the entrepreneurial advice and encouragement always.

To Hailee Justine, for giving me the comfort to leave my day-to-day life to write this book. Your brilliance, commitment and wild-at-heart spirit has gotten us through so much.

To Mae Crowe and Lindsey Hartman, two of the most stylish women I know, for all your behind-the-scenes work to create the visual aesthetic of this book. The photos and illustrations here are a direct result of your incredible eyes.

To Kaela Rodehorst Williams, Hunter Holder, Natalie Mancuso, Tate Tullier, Akasha Rabut and Alicia Parrino for being so generous with your time and talent. The photographs you each take inspire me daily.

To each of my friends and colleagues interviewed here—Suzanne Perron, Lisa Iacono, Hattie Moll, Jolie Bensen Hamilton, Justin Shiels and Amanda deLeon—thank you for sharing your stories and deep love of the city with me.

To Allison Marshall of Rubensteins for sharing the

Rubensteins' story and opening the doors to the store anytime I needed it. New Orleans men continue decade after decade to out-style them all because of you all.

To Micah Haley at *Scene* magazine for giving me my first real writing job in New Orleans and letting my fashion brain take over so many pages of the magazine.

To my fashion week family, your passion and tireless energy to the design community in New Orleans keeps things ticking forward.

To the Hazel girls, for inspiring my own designs and being Louisiana's loveliest of muses.

To the financial supporters of this project: Martine Chaisson Linares, Christopher Brancato, Erin Tufts, Liz Beeson, Candice Hoz, Tate and Sarah Tullier and my grandmother Shirley.

To my best girls for believing that playing dress up is a viable career and supporting one another and me daily.

To Matthew Arthur for being my style partner in crime and my original inspiration to start a fashion career in New Orleans. 'Pagne over pain forever.

To Chelle for being on the same wavelength and, on occasion, in the same time zone.

To my friends, family and confidants for supporting one another's dreams and believing that the Gertrude Stein approach can exist in modern-day New Orleans. The more I allow myself to go into this space of "creating" the more I feel a calmness, but one that exists only in the eye of a storm. If I step one direction to either side, it's back into the whirlwind. What balance it takes, and I'm glad to have each of you standing in it with me.

And lastly, to Micah, who "makes enormous demands on me, does not doubt my courage or my toughness, does not believe me naïve or innocent, [and] has the courage to treat me like a woman." Love you.

INTRODUCTION

When you're traveling, you are what you are right there and then. People
don't have your past to hold against you.
No yesterdays on the road.
—William Least Heat-Moon

Growing up as the oldest child born into a family of travelers I don't remember a time in which the idea of living a nomadic life wasn't in my plan. I never felt settled. I expected, as soon as I was old enough, to take off to live a gypsy life and skip around the world. My grandparents on both sides always had those travel maps full of colorful pins and stories stretched across the walls so that I, by the age of seven, was fully fascinated by the world.

A short story: My French grandmother Norma Louise Tebeau had seven children. After the birth of her sixth, her husband, my grandfather, passed away suddenly. My dad, the oldest of the boys, was twelve. So what did Norma Lou do? Living in Danville, Virginia, there likely weren't a lot of options. So instead, she flew. Literally. She packed up everything, followed some unknown guide in her heart and moved the family to Saigon,

Situated in the French Quarter, the New Orleans Historic Collection is a stunning backdrop for a photo shoot featuring ladies dressed for a tea party. *Jared Hornsby for NOLA Fashion Week.*

Vietnam, to explore an unknown world, language and life.

I always loved her tales of an exotic life in the South Pacific. I'd stay up late listening. The adults, sipping champagne and wine, would switch to French later in the evening, likely to protect virgin ears, and I'd go to bed with a wild imagination dreaming of what their adventures must have been like. I grew up in a family that understands a need to explore. I loved that childhood game where, with one finger on the globe, you close your eyes and spin it, and whatever ends up under your finger when the globe stops is your future destination. As fate would have it, some twenty years later, my spinning globe took me to New Orleans.

When I visited New Orleans for the first time, in the one-hundred-degree temperatures of a July summer day, I was struck immediately by two of the city's usual suspects: the music and the heat.

In New Orleans, at any given hour of the day, music is wafting into the streets. This isn't just a Bourbon Street phenomenon. In fact, the best music in the city is typically tucked away in a side-street venue—string instruments coupled with brass and a mélange of sounds and languages.

And then I felt what most people notice first—it's sweltering. But somehow, to me, it was a comforting heat, like one you might feel after taking one too many shots of tequila or like you'd find on a tropical island during the best vacation you've ever had. There was a breeze coming off the river, my skin glistened the second I stepped outside, and anything but light cotton clothing showed the temperature immediately.

In that visit, I heard the city called "the Northern Most Caribbean City" for the first time, and the name captured me. My nomadic self found this European, African and Caribbean blended city to be home.

It was quite a few years later before I moved to New Orleans. Often I find that, no matter what I'm working on, I get the best results when I torch the standard procedure and start again. The normal stuff bores me and, maybe, scares me. And that is where my love of fashion and style was given wings. I moved to New Orleans working as a senior level executive in the beauty business. However, my muse was always fashion. There's no city that encourages its residents to chase the muse like New Orleans.

Flashback to that same seven-year-old, and this time, I'm in my mother's closet poring through pages of *Vogue* magazine. The photographs, the editors, the designers and the models created a dream world that I wanted so much to be in. I spent my childhood producing "couture" shows modeled after what I learned in the pages of my favorite magazine. I auditioned the girls in the neighborhood and cast them to walk our makeshift catwalks. My style obsession has never been a "study" in the way most people do it—the magazines never leave me once I get my hands on them. Twenty years and a couple hundred pounds of *Vogue* later, I am still studying catwalk, street and market trends. My studio is an explosion of color, vintage fabrics and editorial photo ideas.

Bringing these two loves together, New Orleans and fashion created something fully new for me. In the words of Hemingway, "The world was not wheeling anymore. It was just very clear and bright and inclined to blur at the edges."

This city has given me the opportunity to create a space for my deep adoration of the design process and the artist to live together. New Orleans is a city where artistic survival is an integral part of the community. I hope through the stories ahead, you'll find a kinship to the people, their history and their future.

Opposite: Locally designed and produced garments, from designers Amanda deLeon and Jolie & Elizabeth, are photographed in front of Preservation Hall. *Jared Hornsby for NOLA Fashion Week.*

Part I

A BRIEF HISTORY OF NEW ORLEANS

To get to New Orleans you don't pass through anywhere else. That geographical location, being aloof, lets it hold onto the ritual of its own pace more than other places that have to keep up with the progress.
—Allen Toussaint, musician

We'll begin with a jaunt through the history of New Orleans because, of course, before we can talk about style, and specifically style in the Crescent City, we should take a stroll through the city itself, get to know it a bit, as well as those who love it and its deep roots.

New Orleans is one of the world's most captivating cities.

Stroll through the French Quarter on any given evening, and the presence of history is felt everywhere. Bartenders serve absinthe cocktails in Pirates Alley, and clairvoyant palm readers make their living in the shadows of the glorious St. Louis Cathedral, founded in 1720 as a Catholic parish and the oldest cathedral in the country. Directly outside the

The Jackson Monument and St. Louis Cathedral, located in the heart of the French Quarter, face the Mississippi River and are surrounded by historic buildings, including the Presbytere, the Cabildo and the Lower and Upper Pontalba Apartments, the oldest apartments in the United States. *Library of Congress, Prints & Photographs Division, Detroit Publishing Company Collection, [LC-D418-8106].*

cathedral walls, the neighboring alley is home to the ghost of Père Antoine—or that's at least the claim of locals and tourists alike.[2] Antoine was the pastor of the then St. Louis Church. He baptized the High Voodoo Priestess (and liquor importer) Marie Laveaux—and performed her wedding Mass, for that matter—right there in the Roman Catholic Archdiocese of New Orleans.

New Orleans is a city steeped in interestingly bold juxtapositions. Pirates and priests sit side by side in the city's massive cemeteries; funerals are celebrated with dancing in the streets; and the rich influences from Europe, the Caribbean, Africa and beyond create a fully diverse melting pot of food, music, culture and fashion. On the surface level, it's a city of the usual suspects: daiquiris, beads on Bourbon, po' boys, red beans and rice, jazz music floating into the streets and street performers working for change. But to get there, we'll start with a play by play of how the Big Easy came to be.

Café Du Monde in 1973, a popular destination for locals and tourists, is located next to the French Market and home to the famous New Orleans café au lait and beignet. *Barbara Ann Spengler via Flickr.*

1

THE GATHERING OF WATERS

*All good New Orleanians go to look at the Mississippi
at least once a day. At night it is like creeping into a
dark bedroom to look at a sleeping child—something of
that sort—gives you the same warm nice feeling, I mean.*
—Sherwood Anderson

It all started with a river. What bustles now with commerce and recreation, steamboats and barges, stories and songs was twenty-five thousand years ago a sheet of ice that covered the North American continent.

As the ice melted, it flowed south, a simple act of the Earth's gravitational pull, and the delta filled. As the sea retreated, five thousand years ago, the first child of the Mississippi was born, her name: Lake Pontchartrain. Between the lake and the river, swampland emerged full of cottonmouth snakes, bullfrogs, alligators and nutria rats (appealing neighbors, no?) that would eventually become New Orleans.[3]

The river itself, more than anything, determined the location, dimension, architecture and lifestyle of the city. Presently, the city is sinking at a rate of three inches per century, and over time, the residents of the city, who sometimes could care to notice, have adjusted to their water-locked environment because, well, what else could they do? Except for the levees, there are no

View across the Mississippi River into the Vieux Carre from Algiers Point. *Lithograph from Henry Lewis, "New Orleans," in* Das Illustrirte Mississippithal: Dargestellt in 80 Nach der Natur Aufgenommenen *(Düsseldorf, Germany: Arnz & Company, 1857) via Archive.org and the University of Pittsburgh Library System.*

natural land surfaces that are higher than fifteen feet above sea level; that's the height of an extra tall first-floor apartment building ceiling, and for comparison, the only other locations in all of the United States with this same phenomenon are Death Valley[4] and the Salton Sink in California.[5]

Today's tourists will find immediate familiarity in things like a typical dress-in-green Saint Patrick's Day parade (although, in the Irish Channel, the celebration goes on for days), soul food restaurants with long waits for traditional cooking (however, New Orleans Faubourg Tremé claims several of the country's absolute best), African American storefront churches and southern-style architecture featuring porticos and peristyle; however, the usual visitors, American ones especially, are often surprised to find that much of the city functions more like a European city than an

The forty-two cemeteries in New Orleans all have aboveground vaults, a Spanish custom and necessity because of the high water table. W.T. Lee, "Tombs," U.S. Department of the Interior U.S. Geological Survey 1916.

American one. While it's often called a foreign place, it isn't. It's solidly an American city with plenty of American traditions spinning from it, even if it's a very different American place with a peculiar history.

New Orleans is a place where Native American Indians intermingled with Europeans and shared their cultures and traditions with the Africans. The early French government encouraged friendship and connectivity; the French game plan for producing a lasting culture in an extraordinarily challenging environment marked New Orleans as highly unique from its inception.[8]

2

THE EXPLORER, THE FRIENDS AND THE BROTHERS

In today's world of Google maps, GPS and Siri, it's sometimes hard to imagine what the early explorers must have gone through. Those attempting to conquer the Mississippi believed it flowed east to west, and since they were on a quest for China, it seemed to be the perfect route. So how did New Orleans go from a mosquito-filled marshland to a stylishly cool and creative world destination? Well, that's where these characters come in.

The Explorer: Hernando de Soto

The first of the explorers to lay eyes on the mighty Mississippi was the governor of Cuba, Hernando de Soto, in 1538. De Soto was on a mission for one thing, like so many of the explorers, and that mission was gold. He set out with 620 men, 223 horses, hogs, bloodhounds, firearms, cannons and steel armor.[9]

Two years into his mission, he arrived on the Mississippi with little care for the "majesty or beauty of this river." He had a burning desire for gold, and only gold, similar to the want of quite a few New Orleans fashionistas whom we'll meet later in this story. He commanded his men: "Let us hasten and build boats that we may cross."[10] It wasn't easy. The river is wide and rough, and with zero knowledge of what they were dealing with, it took some time. But finally, success!—they crossed. But what did they find once they arrived on the other side? Nothing. No gold and an unhappy De Soto.

For another year, they wandered west. Their experience was that of the standard explorer clichés. They fought with some Indians while others loved them—one group even thought De Soto was a god, on a mission to heal the sick. De Soto, not being a god, was quite a disappointment.[11] They lost men to disease, and they used up their supplies too quickly. Over the course of their travels and camping in less-than-ideal environments, De Soto's health took a turn for the worse. With nothing to show for his mission and with a shaken spirit, he knew his time was up. He gathered his remaining men and asked their forgiveness for leading them into treachery and suffering, and then, the next day, he was dead and buried at the swampy camp.

Upon his death, his crew had an immediate fear that the Indians would revolt against them should they discover that De Soto was in fact mortal: being everlasting kept him and, now more importantly, his men safe. They couldn't

There is a unique bond between the land and the people in the Crescent City. Everyone here came from somewhere else, the muddy brown current of life prying them loose from their homeland and sweeping them downstream, bumping and scraping, until they got caught by the horseshoe bend that is New Orleans. Every single person walking, living and loving in the city is a refugee from somewhere else. But they made something unique, the people and the land, when they came together in that cohesive, magnetic, magical spot; this sediment of society made something that is not French, not Spanish, and incontrovertibly not American.

—James Caskey

risk De Soto's death being found out; so a night later, his body was pulled right back up from the swamp, weighed down with sand and stones and sent off in the middle of the very river that he'd discovered.[12]

The Friends: La Salle and Tonti

Next up, we have the gentlemen René-Robert Cavelier, Sieur de La Salle, and his friend Henri de Tonti. Also en route toward what they assumed was the Pacific Ocean, with permissions and directives from Louis XIV of France, La Salle and Tonti were on a hunt for land to colonize in the New World and, in turn, gain further prestige for France as a world power. France had little money for such expeditions, so La Salle paid to have his own ship built, led a group down the river and, within two months, arrived in the Gulf of Mexico traveling from the Illinois River. Voilà! Upon his arrival, he claimed the area for France and named it Louisiana in honor of his king.

Henri de Tonti was La Salle's best friend and confidant. He documented the trip through personal journals and letters to friends. La Salle and Tonti were ambitious gents. They reveled in the idea of building a river highway and trade routes expanding wider than La Salle's home country. After their arrival, low on supplies and in no condition to set up the New World they were imagining, La Salle headed off to France to get all the things his new colony and settlers would require.

La Salle wrangled four ships, marines, soldiers and 250 settlers while in France and went straight back across the Atlantic to return to his new home of Louisiana. On the way, however, he stopped over in Santo Domingo, and then, rather than taking the same route that he knew down the Mississippi River, he made a fatal decision to approach from the south. The uncharted bayous, swamps, sandbars and estuaries that surely all looked alike coming from a ship sailing into the Gulf of Mexico thwarted La Salle's efforts. He had absolutely no point of reference coming from the south and, seven months later, landed on a Texas bay. He was wise enough to know that he'd overshot his trajectory and had royally screwed up this one. Things only worsened from there. In a one-two-three—well, four—punch, his ship's captain abandoned him, he lost a second ship to the Spanish in the Gulf and a third in the Texas bay and finally wrecked number four in a storm. Then, his own men murdered him and went on to Canada telling the story of "La Salle's Folly."[13]

In the meantime, La Salle's forever-friend Tonti heard the news of La Salle's attempt to travel in from the south and headed out to a predetermined rendezvous point between what would become New Orleans and Baton Rouge. Tonti left behind a letter for La Salle (who of course would never receive it) with an Indian chieftain.

Fourteen years later, in 1699, that letter was delivered to the hands of brothers Jean-Baptiste Le Moyne, Sieur de Bienville, and Pierre le Moyne, Sieur d'Iberville.[14]

The Brothers: Iberville and Bienville

Iberville, the older of the two brothers, presented a renewed plan to their French king to develop a colony on the mouth of the Mississippi. Again with approval from Louis XIV, the explorers were off to the races. Iberville found a sponsor and, along with his younger brother, two war ships, two freighters and a group of settlers and marines, headed out to make a go at settling Louisiana. On the way, they made a pit stop in Mobile Bay, got directions from the Indians and then island hopped across Dauphin and Ship Islands before arriving at the mouth of the river on March 2, 1699. The following day was Shrove Tuesday, and as the brothers traveled north into the bayou, they held a small celebration, named their discovery Mardi Gras Bayou and effectively established the Mardi Gras holiday in Louisiana.

The following Sunday, post Mass, Iberville wrote in his journal about the discovery of Tonti's time capsule–like correspondence for La Salle. The Mougoulacha chief, upon meeting Bienville, passed the fourteen-year-old letter to him and, according to Iberville, removed all doubt that the Malbanchia is the Mississippi.[15]

The letter closed with Tonti's expression of disappointment of not finding his mate La Salle: "Though we have gotten no information of you nor found any trace of you, I do not despair that God will grant a full success to your business and your enterprise. I hope this with all my heart, for you have not a more faithful follower than I, who sacrifices everything to seek you."[16] The letter, an unbelievable and fateful find so many years later, sealed the deal for Iberville. They'd most certainly found "La Salle's River."

Once the brothers had settled, Iberville departed for France, leaving Bienville behind at the fort at Biloxi. Bienville set out regularly to explore their newfound home on the Mississippi. On one particularly eventful afternoon, he encountered the *Carolina Galley*, an English ship packed to the brim with settlers intending to colonize the area for themselves. Bienville, in one of the biggest bluffs in history, gave the ranking British officer phony directions and warned of all sorts of French forts ahead. The officer bought it, hook, line and sinker, and promptly turned the brigade in the other direction. Had that officer not believed Bienville's fib, the English could have headed directly up the river and settled New Orleans. The site of that infamous meeting is English Turn, ten miles south of New Orleans. This was the first of many times in which the British were turned back from Bienville's New Orleans.

Iberville returned a year later with a crew of street thieves, women of the night, prisoners and debtors—quite the crowd to settle France's new find. Iberville assigned command of Fort Maurepas and Ocean Springs to twenty-one-year-old Bienville. But then the acting head of the Louisiana territory died, and Bienville promptly became the new commander. Iberville, the true father of Louisiana, died in Havana in 1706 of yellow fever, elevating Bienville again, this time to governor of Louisiana.[17]

Bienville had his work cut out for him. This wasn't going to be an easy gig. Provisions from France were sparse, and his only good option, meaning the option to keep his best people alive, was to send them out to live with the Indians. The Indians were friends to Bienville. They kept the Frenchmen well fed and gave them shelter, and in exchange, the French shared their love of festivity, dance and song and, of course, the French language.

From here we'll move ahead with a timeline of the events that land us directly on the founding of the city of New Orleans.

1707: Operating on limited supplies, Bienville runs into trouble for selling supplies for six times their worth. France, none too happy with this finding, sends in a replacement governor, who dies en route. Bienville loses his position, and promptly gains it right back.

1708: Land concessions begin in the area that will become New Orleans. The concessions were narrow, extending only from Bayou St. John to Bayou Gentilly.

1712: The colony, which still isn't self-sufficient, is transferred to a banker, Antoine Crozat. Crozat, making decisions from afar, replaces Bienville with the founder of Detroit—Sieur de Cadillac. Cadillac creates an instantaneous divide between the Louisiana colonists and the Indians, which doesn't fare well for anyone.

1716: The first Natchez War breaks out. Cadillac, having no cultural understanding of the Indians, created the whole upset by neglecting to make peace with the Natchez. Literally, he snubbed them when he didn't take part in smoking the peace calumet with them, which would effectively have renewed their alliance. The Natchez react to Cadillac's slight by killing four French traders. Bienville is sent to fight against his old friends and tricks the Natchez leaders into a not-so-friendly parley, in which he ambushes and retains the culprits who attacked his own people.

1717: Crozat, losing money hand over fist on the investment, transfers the colony and its seven hundred people to a company called "Company of the West," owned by known murderer and gambler John Law. The company launches a fierce marketing initiative throughout France, Germany

and Switzerland that exaggerates the riches and glamour of Louisiana. The company offers up stories of gold, pearls and a fountain of youth to voluntary immigrants. In the meantime, the paupers, prisoners and prostitutes are continually shipped over, growing quite an interesting population.

1718: Bienville, steadfast in his dream, establishes Nouvelle Orleans, Louisiana. He, ever the determined one, convinced the royal engineer and his team that the spot in the middle of a cypress swamp, teeming with mosquitoes, alligators and intense tropical heat and on the grounds of the Chitimacha Indians—where Esplanade Avenue sits today—was "the best [place] to locate the settlement."[18] Midway through the year, the first wave of immigrants responding to the ad campaign arrived into the new city, and overnight the population doubled.[19]

3
THE CRESCENT CITY IS BORN

*America has only three cities: New York, San Francisco,
and New Orleans. Everywhere else is Cleveland.*
                    —Tennessee Williams

So how do we jump from Bienville's dream to the American city New Orleans has become today, referred to as the northernmost Caribbean city with a deep and soulful richness where Africans, both slave and free people of color, and American Indians blended their cultures with the original French settlers and then the Spanish, Irish, Germans, Cubans, Haitians and all those to come?[20]

The French were responsible for the foundation of the city, and the initial conditions of encouraging relationships between the natives, the settlers and free and enslaved Africans established quite the cultural backbone. Adrien de Pauger, the royal engineer, laid out Bienville's New Orleans in full. The streets of the Vieux Carré were arranged strategically in a boxy grid pattern, rather than conforming to the serpent-like shape of the river. The streets were named for the royal houses of France as well as Catholic saints.

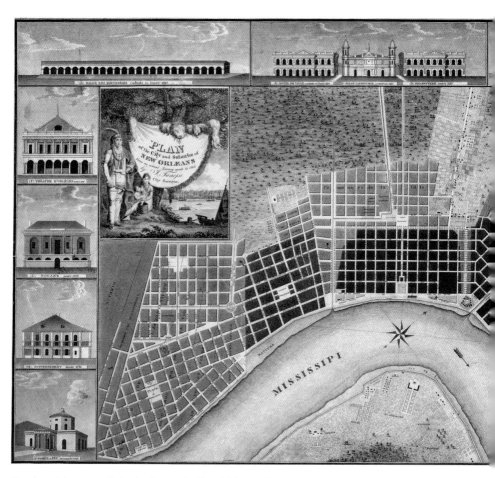

This plan of the city and suburbs depicts the French Market, Charity Hospital, the Ursuline Convent, the Cabildo and theaters. *Charles Del Vecchio and P. Maspero,* Plan of the City of and Suburbs of New Orleans, *Mounted cloth relief,* Library of Congress, Geography and Maps Division, loc.gov.

The Spanish then took possession of Louisiana with the signing of the Treaty of Fontainebleau, and although the treaty was kept secret to all but the Spanish for several years, the first major social transformation since the founding of the city followed. The reign of the Spaniards was short, but one of the most important contributions was the building codes enacted that spared the Vieux Carré from the fires that swept the city in 1788 and again in 1794. Architectural trademarks of the area often attributed to the French, including the ornate wrought-iron balconies, are actually Spanish contributions.

In the table on page 42, you can find a short run down of what came from each culture.[21]

Additional contributors followed, including the Irish, Germans, Acadians, Haitians (who brought

FRENCH	SPANISH
city plan	architecture of the Vieux Carré
cooking with butter, crème and chicory coffee	cooking with olive oil and wine
the Code Noir	Manumission
par terre gardens of the French Quarter	arabesque ironwork, covered passages and arches
the Faubourgs and Jackson Square	the cemeteries and St. Charles Ave
Ursuline Nuns	first Catholic bishop

voodoo and rum), Hondurans, Italians, Greeks, Croatians, Cubans and Filipinos. The Irish and Germans specifically made New Orleans one of the main immigrant ports in the country, second only to New York and far ahead of other northern cities like Boston and Philadelphia. A current visitor may wonder about the Brooklyn- or Chicagoan-like dialects heard in various neighborhoods. These are a direct reflection of Irish, German and Italian immigration. Then there's the Cajun integration into the daily speak. The Acadian immigrants, or Cajuns, were ousted from their native Nova Scotia by the British and settled the bayou country just west of New Orleans. Just before the beginning of the twentieth century, thousands of Sicilians came into New Orleans and added further complexity to the already highly diverse population. Those coming from Catholic Mediterranean countries furthered the divide between New Orleanians and the other southern Protestant cities.[22]

Above: Garments from local designers Amanda deLeon and Jolie & Elizabeth are photographed in front of Preservation Hall for a NOLA Fashion Week marketing campaign. *Jared Hornsby for NOLA Fashion Week.*

Opposite: Garments from local designer Matthew Arthur, a *Project Runway* cast member, are photographed at the Historic New Orleans Collection. *Jared Hornsby for NOLA Fashion.*

And then there came the Creoles. The word *Creole* is derived from the Spanish *criollo*, which means a child born in the colonies. By this definition, any child born in New Orleans, of either Spanish or French descent, would be considered a Creole, even if his or her parents were strictly European. The Creole society was a mash up of French aristocrats, merchants, soldiers, farmers, African and Caribbean slaves and free people of color. It was the trend of the time for the Creole aristocratic gentlemen to

take black or mixed-race mistresses. Absolutely unheard of in other North American colonial cities, the mistresses, and the children from these unions, were treated well and often given European educations and property for their future lives.[23]

Part II

NEW ORLEANS HISTORIC STYLE

4

New Orleans Heritage

To begin a conversation about the sartorial nature of New Orleans—and there is most certainly a whole lot of it—we'll spend some time discussing the styles and the stories of the trendsetters unique to this city. From Wynton Marsalis, Jedi master–level jazz musician and current artistic director at Lincoln Center, to nineteenth-century actress, painter and poet Adah Menken, highest paid actress in her time and made famous for a stage performance in which she rode horseback nude, and Miss New Orleans 1931, Dorothy Lamour, who became a Hollywood actress and World War II glamour girl, the aesthetics and fashion sense of New Orleans natives range from fresh and cool to quirky and eccentric. Coupled with the costumes and couture of Mardi Gras, as well as festival fashions, the diversity of style is as wide as that of the city's people.

Opposite, top: Actress and performance artist Adah Menken is in her true to fashion-exhibitionist form in these images. *Library of Congress Prints & Photographs Division.*

Opposite, bottom: A Creole beauty: actress, singer and Miss New Orleans 1931 Dorothy Lamour. CINELANDIA *magazine.*

The Baleine Brides and the Casket Girls

As John Law's marketing campaign continued to attract early settlers to New Orleans, there was quickly a disproportionate number of unmarried men to women. Bienville called back to Paris for help. His men, he said, were "running in the woods after Indian girls."[24] The solution was simple. Paris needed to send over ladies suitable to become wives. The first round of gals between the ages of twelve and twenty-five, "the *Baleine* Brides," named for the ship in which they traveled on, were sent on their way. The Brides, arriving in 1721, didn't exactly answer Bienville's call after having traveled across the ocean in less-than-lovely conditions. Ten of the initial eighty-eight women died before actually becoming brides, and of those who lived, only nineteen found husbands. The challenge, of course, with the remaining fifty-nine gals, was that they were quite rowdy. Why? Because where does one find women to ship across the Atlantic

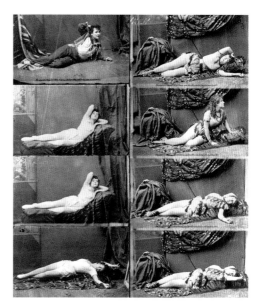

CINELANDIA

PUBLICADA EN HOLLYWOOD

ABRIL, 1944

DOROTHY
LAMOUR
Paramount

LOS PREMIOS DE
LA ACADEMIA

LOS ASTROS EN CASA
CARAS NUEVAS

Ocean to a New World? Well, in this case, they came from a Parisian correctional house for young women, and they were truly in no mood to be settled.

The bawdy brides were distinctly different from the next group, the "Casket Girls."[25] While the Brides were considered undesirables, in 1728, the new group was quite different. The Girls, rather than being street vagrants and wild women, were recruited from orphanages and convents, practically guaranteeing that they were well-behaved virgins.[26] Victor Hebert's musical *Naughty Marietta*, the fictional account of a runaway who came to New Orleans via an escape at Mozambique, was inspired by the story of the Casket Girls.

There is a further distinction between the types of women sent to New Orleans. Those called "King's Daughters" were sent at the expense of the king versus women who voluntarily immigrated. The Casket Girls were sent by the king's orders, and those of higher family status were often matched with officers and gentlemen; the sponsoring of women to come to the New World from this point forward was an initiative all across New France, from Canada to Louisiana.[27]

New Orleanians love a good tale, and the rumors and speculation about the subversive nature of many of the women have created fantastic stories. Some say the women were actually vampires (how on trend!). The signs were certainly there. Many of the women became so sick during their transport that they arrived in New

Orleans skeletal and pale—there weren't exactly fine meals and sundecks on the ships. Some, in their travels, contracted tuberculosis with its telltale sign of coughing blood—definitely a sign of a vampire! Then, there was the name of the bag they carried: "the casket." While it makes for a good story to think they were traveling with some sort of coffin, the name actually comes from *casquette*—a simple overnight bag, smaller than a chest, in which to carry their few possessions.[28]

So what was the general fashion and dress of the King's Daughters, who traveled with just an overnight bag across the ocean? Well, it was the 1700s, so they weren't exactly packing like the ladies traveling on the future Olympic-class ocean liners. Most of the women arrived with just one change of clothes and a bag packed full of household items so that she could set up housekeeping for her new husband.[29]

The women certainly would have loved to emulate the Regency and Rococo fashions, and once they were married, they were able to acquire more things. They often wore pastels imitating the styles of the king and his court. Pastels also served a purpose in New Orleans, as lighter fabrics were necessary because of the extreme heat. The French Revolution marked the end of brocade dresses, powdered wigs and heels in Paris, and the style in Paris influenced the style in the New World as well. The new fashions included buoyant skirts that floated above layers of petticoats and corsets tightened below plunging necklines, creating sensual hourglass figures. While Parisian women of status enjoyed luxury fabrics and dresses made of silks and velvets with embellished embroideries, the bourgeois women made due with cotton and wool of the same shape.

The Ursuline Nuns and the Sisters
of the Holy Family

The next style setters in New Orleans were the Ursuline Nuns. Nuns? Absolutely. Their impact on the early settlers of New Orleans was widespread. They offered free classes for all people—slaves, Creoles and Native Americans alike—established a social welfare center and opened a hospital, in which they treated everyone from slaves who had contracted yellow fever to soldiers suffering from war injuries. They also opened the first school of music and the first boarding school, and then, in 1927, two hundred years after their arrival in New Orleans, the Ursuline opened the Ursuline College on St. Charles Avenue.

Their attire included the standard black dress, and what fashionista doesn't love a quality black dress? Their dress was bound by a leather girdle, a black sleeveless cloak and a close-fitting headdress with a white veil and was finished with a longer black veil. The first Ursuline Nuns traveled to New Orleans on a five-month journey as directed by King Louis XV with a three-part game plan. Their first mission was to establish a hospital for the poor and sick, their second to create a European-style educational program for the young girls being born to the wealthier of the settlers and their third to save the heathen souls of the Louisiana Indians running about in the swamps.

Arriving in 1727, the nuns set up shop at the Old Ursuline Convent in the Vieux Carré, the first building in the region. Today, the Ursuline Academy is the oldest continually operating Catholic school and school for girls in the country.[30]

Another group of holy women arose about one hundred years after the Ursulines arrived in New Orleans. The Sisters of the Holy Family were the first African American Catholics to serve as missionaries. The Sisters of the Holy Family not only cared for slaves, free people of color, orphans and the elderly but were also responsible for looking after the quadroon women.

A depiction of a nun and a child from the Sisterhood of the Holy Family, founded by Abbe Rousselon in 1835. *Winter Halder, "A Colored Sister of the Creole Family" in* The Picayune's Guide to New Orleans, *5th ed. (New Orleans, LA: The Picayune, 1903), 22.*

Nuns buying fruit at the French Market. At the south end of the French Quarter, the market is a tourist and local destination for produce, gifts and local wares. *Library of Congress Prints & Photographs Division.*

The Quadroon Women

The word *quadroon* comes from the French term *quarteron* and the Spanish *cuarterón*, both meaning fourth. A quadroon person would be of biracial descent with one African grandparent and three Caucasian grandparents.[31]

"No section of New Orleans is invested with more romance than the square," in which the Orleans Theatre home to the Quadroon Ballroom stood. The balls were celebrated throughout the world. With olive skin and the "deeply increased brilliance of the eye,"[32] the quadroon women were considered some of the most beautiful in the world.

In an interview, Tulane historian Dr. Emily Clark described the American quadroon women:

> *There are really two versions. One is the virtually unknown historical reality, the married free women of color of New Orleans who were paragons of piety and respectability. The other is the more familiar mythic figure who took shape in the antebellum American imagination. If you asked a white nineteenth-century American what a quadroon was, they would answer that she was a light-skinned free woman of color who preferred being the mistress of a white man to marriage with a man who shared her racial ancestry.*
>
> *In order to ensnare white lovers who would provide for them, quadroons were supposedly schooled from girlhood by their mothers to be virtuosos in the erotic arts. When they came of age, their mothers put them on display at quadroon balls and negotiated a contract with a white lover to set the young woman up in a house and provide enough*

money to support her and any children born of the liaison. The arrangement usually ended in heartbreak for the quadroon when the lover left her to marry a white woman. There is one other key characteristic of the mythic American Quadroon: she was to be found only in New Orleans.[33]

The descriptions of what the quadroon women actually wore to balls varies considerably. One early description from a German count notes the whole affair as a rather tame one. The young women were "well and gracefully dressed, and conducted themselves with much propriety and modesty. Cotillions and waltzes were danced, and several of the ladies performed elegantly."[34] Just a decade later, however, a visitor from Virginia described the scene as quite a spectacle: ladies dancing in their nightclothes creating sexual fantasies for the white men attending the event. As time went on, the balls moved from their original home to raucous dance halls down by the riverside. In all cases, the relationships these women created with the white men allowed for economic stability, and according to Clark, New Orleans, and most certainly its style, "is itself seen by the rest of the country as a quadroon, a city given over to the exotic, transgressive qualities that defined the myth."[35]

The Storyville Women

"Streetwalkers ply the boulevards of every major U.S. city, but there has been only one time and place in U.S. history where legal prostitution flourished in an open, competitive urban environment: the Storyville section of New Orleans from January I, 1898, until November 12, 1917."[36]

Storyville, the red-light district of New Orleans, was established on July 6, 1897, in an attempt by the New Orleans City Council, led by Sidney Story, to control the city's rampant prostitution problem. Story's idea was that by legalizing prostitution and limiting it to a thirty-eight-block area on the edge of the French Quarter, the problem would at least be contained and perhaps regulated. Story certainly didn't intend to glamorize prostitution or create an almost celebrity-like status for the women working in the district, which is effectively what happened.

Mansions, saloons and low-cost "cribs" lined the streets of Storyville. The environment was highly profitable, entrepreneurial and competitive, and it existed for almost twenty years right in the central city of New Orleans. A directory of the area in 1915 listed 773 total women, of those 425 white, 251 black and 9 octoroon. The directory also included 72 white cabaret dancers and 16 of color.[37]

Property owners, madams, liquor retailers and other anonymous interested parties published guides, known as "Blue Books," similar to what could be found in Paris or London sharing the who's who and what's where of the red-light district. In New Orleans, the books were published on the second floor of a brothel owned and operated by a madam by the name of Lulu White. The books included advertisements taken out by the madams running the bordellos and included images and descriptions of the most notorious prostitutes. The books showed lavish interiors, leopard-skin rugs, ivory ornaments, golden candelabras and plush furniture and often boasted of the variety of amenities provided by the house. The books included ads for liquor, beer and, out of necessity, cures for sexually transmitted diseases.

Lulu White's Mahogany Hall was on the cover of one of the books and was described as having fifteen bedrooms, five parlors, hot and cold water baths, elevators built for two, steam heat and marble floors.[38]

Miss Lulu, as she was called, was a woman of West Indies descent and was described as having shiny black hair and the bluest eyes. She only housed the fairest of girls born and bred in Louisiana. She stayed in trouble with the law, although most of her on-the-record offenses were related to serving booze without a permit. She was also known to be violent when patrons threatened her business or the girls whom she employed.[39]

Another notable house was that of Miss Willie Piazza. Miss Willie's was a house for octoroon girls. She proudly advertised that her girls were the best singers and dancers and could cure any case of blues. The "Countess," as Willie was often called, was quite the fashion plate. She, of course, had no claim to such a regal title, but she nonetheless certainly dressed as if she did. She wore diamond chokers, smoked imported cigarettes in a two-foot ivory, gold and diamond holder and wore a monocle on her eye. When out on the town, attending shows at the French Opera House or the Fair Grounds racetrack, she often passed for white. She was truly a style leader of her time. Many matriarchs of the first families of New Orleans, taking note of Miss Willie's style, attended city

Fourteen-year-old Louis Dupree, a Western Union messenger, on the routes of the Storyville red-light district. *Library of Congress, Prints & Photographs Division, National Child Labor Committee Collection, [LC-DIG-nclc-03922].*

events "with their dressmakers in tow just to copy the outfits worn by Countess Willie and her girls."[40]

As travelers arrived in New Orleans on the Southern Railroad Station, Storyville was often their first introduction to the city. The lower-class cribs, which often had no plumbing and rented for twenty cents per night, were first; then the higher-class brothels, some of which were three stories tall, keeping dozens upon dozens of women employed; and then right down the road from the train station sat Arlington Annex, the main saloon of the unofficial "mayor of Storyville," Tom Anderson. The saloon and the brothels served as musical hubs as well, with the likes of jazz musicians Jelly Roll Morton, Kid Orly, Mutt Carey and King Oliver all beginning their careers there. Anderson, a state legislator and an oil company head, was the boss of the district.

One of the most intriguing characters of the Storyville era, was the French Creole and French Quarter native, E.J. Bellocq. Bellocq was a professional photographer, hired to take photos of landmarks, ships and machinery for local companies. By night, however, Bellocq had quite a different artistic passion. After

Opposite: A New Orleans Storyville prostitute in her fancy stockings is giving a toast to photographer E.J. Bellocq. *John Ernest Joespeh Bellocq, "Untitled," photograph, 1912, New Orleans.*

his death, a significant number of some of the most seditious photos of the times surfaced in his studio. The photos are haunting and intimate images of the Storyville prostitutes. Sometimes nude, sometimes extravagantly dressed and sometimes somewhere in between, each photo has a chilling feel of mystery. When the negatives were found, in many cases, the faces of the subjects had been scratched out and defaced, adding to the mystique of the photos. The girls whom Bellocq photographed were typically on the expensive, higher-class end. We know so because of their fancy stockings and elaborate underclothing. Bellocq's photos are the best record of not only the tradeswomen of Storyville themselves but also of the interiors of the brothels.

The prostitutes of the Storyville-era brothels were unintentional—maybe sometimes intentional—trendsetters for the high-society women. Initially, the prostitutes emulated the women of wealth. But over time, the glamorized image of the prostitute, which combined fantasy and reality, caught the eye of the respectable women.[41]

Opposite: Storyville ladies in plush surroundings bide time with a card game between clients. John Ernest Joespeh Bellocq, *"Girls Playing Cards, Storyville,"* photograph, 1911–13, New Orleans.

The brothel madams took notice that the young American men were attracted to the high-heeled boots that the French girls wore. They took initiative to import the footwear for their girls, which led to an interest from the local high-society women. The first American high-heel shoe factory opened in 1888, imitating the French shoe design, and as the trend grew, the fashion shoe industry in America was born.[42]

While the madams used fancy shoes and clothes as a strategy to lure in the local men and traveling gents, the society wives employed the same tactic to keep their men at home:

> *According to nineteenth-century magazines, it was a woman's duty to make that home such a haven of beauty, order, and domestic peace that the men who lived there could never be lured away to drink and gamble (or worse) in bars and clubs. As the central figure of that home, the woman herself must also be beautiful—or at least beautifully dressed—and pretty shoes were part of her allure.* Demorest's Monthly Magazine *warned its middle-class readers in 1883 that "the chasseur is another item of the home dress, which should never be neglected, for it is certain never to escape observation. A shrewd writer says, 'Many a man's heart has been kept from*

*wandering by the bow on his wife's slipper.'
Daintily dressed feet are always admired, so
we would advise all young wives, and older
ones, too, for that matter, to look well to the
ways of their feet and dress them in pretty
house and neat slippers."*[43]

The Storyville girls over time became aware of the competition with the respectable American women. In the words of one of the prostitutes, "All them gals was dressed up to kill in silks and satins and they had all their mens dressed up, too. So, we figures and figures how we could go and show them whores up with our frocks."[44] Women on both sides of the tracks, it seems, were using sexualized forms of dress to grow, or in some cases keep, their social position.

So who were the women who took up the trade? In most cases, women had three life options: marry (the obvious first choice), be a poor relative (not glamorous but at least respectable) or sell oneself in order to survive. For women who didn't come from wealth, attracting an affluent husband required a wardrobe that allowed her to pass as if she were from similar background.[45] Lucy Hooper, an American writer, claimed that many women entered prostitution for the love of the clothing. They'd worked in low-paying jobs—such as shop clerks or in factories, where wages were as low as three dollars a week—and dreamed of a better life. One respectable working girl considering her options was quoted as saying, "I thought all the time of the money I could make and the fine clothes I could have [as a prostitute]."[46]

The *Mascot*, a New Orleans weekly newspaper specializing in gossip, sensationalism and general mudslinging, placed the blame for leading women into prostitution in the hands of the city's milliners and dressmakers:

> *It is on record, however, and there are now fallen women, who have been led astray while employed by milliners and dressmakers who make a specialty of just such a class of customers. There is hardly a single dressmaker or milliner in New Orleans who do* [sic] *not pursue such practices. If there are, we would take pleasure in printing their names. We make no exceptions in this matter and mention no name particularly because everyone of them is included in this generality.*[47]

The process of obtaining their ball gowns was an entertaining diversion for the Storyville girls. "Shopping was almost sexualized, fetishistically, as women who had 'fallen' spoke of the irresistible touch of silk and satin, the visual seduction of the displays, and their thirst for possession."[48] Rosa, a New Orleans prostitute, described the New Orleans shopping procedure like this:

> Sawmtime we get up early, go by Canal Street an' look in de staws. Ees manny t'ings een de staws an' we got plenny mawney you know for buy annyt'ing; but clothes, mos' de time we buy from salesmens dey come from Nort'. De salesmen, you know, dey got t'ings, more how you say up-to-date. May Spencer she's tell us salesman he gon' be dere Sawnday ten o'clock in de mawning we get up early we get dress to see clothes…De salesman he tak' orders he write een hees book. May Spencer she pay faw everyt'ing, and den she tak' back a leetle every week unteel ees enough mawney. All de womens dey see us een Canal Street dey look on our dresses an' dey know dey deen come from no staws een New Orleans, so dey know we all pu-ta-but we don' care.[49]

The prostitutes of the most expensive houses pored over elaborate gowns that the peddlers brought. They drove around the city wearing diamond rings, tiaras and stacks of bracelets, always in hats and gloves, enjoying a shared sense of wealth and status as the local elite.[50]

On the opposite end of the spectrum, the women working in the lowest-level cribs, or even outside the district illegally, had a very different style of attire. These prostitutes had a couple options. The first was the dowdy "Mother Hubbard" dress. Originally used by

THE FASHION

DEFIANCE CIGAR MANUFACTORY

D.H. & Co.

missionaries, the dress draped loosely and fell all the way past the ankles to the floor. The second option was called the "Chippie"—which was noted by Jelly Roll Morton: "The chippies in their little-girl dresses standing in the crib doors."[51] The Chippie mimicked a style that a child would wear with a short skirt and little fabric: "Previously, only dresses for very young girls had exposed so much of these limbs."[52]

Respectable women, just as before, followed along as the Chippie dress and the silk lingerie–style of dress worn by both lower- and higher-class girls became a trend. "Dainty undergarments," it was decided, were no longer a sign of depravity.[53] Since the time of the Storyville, it's interesting to note that beauty routines that were at that time considered "whorish"—applying rouge and lipstick, donning a wig or altering hair length and shaving one's legs—are now considered American beauty standards.[54]

Opposite: This advertisement depicts the power of "The Fashion" from the Defiance Cigar Manufactory. *"The Fashion Cigar Trademark," Department of the Treasury, Customs Service, Collection District of New Orleans (Louisiana). (1804-1913).*

5

THE HABERDASHERIES, MILLINERS AND FINERY OF A RETAIL DISTRICT

Following the French tradition of grandiose shopping and beautiful department stores, it makes perfect sense that by the early nineteenth century, New Orleans would be considered the most fashionable shopping destination in the South. Over the next one hundred years, New Orleans–based retail stores stocked the finest fabrics, hired tailors to customize garments for their clients, employed milliners at the top of their trade and designed exotic perfumes for the highest-society locals and visitors. The retail shops running from Canal Street down into the French Quarter spoiled and indulged the discerning shoppers looking for only the best.

D.H. Holmes:
The Foundation of a Retail District

D.H. Holmes, styled after a Parisian department store, became the anchor of the fashion and retail district.

Opposite: The famous Katz & Besthoff drugstore, shown here in its early days, was headquartered on Canal Street. *Louisiana Division/City Archives, New Orleans Public Library.*

The Canal Street flagship location of Maison Blanche was one of the finest and most extravagant department stores in the South. *Library of Congress, Prints & Photographs Division, Detroit Publishing Company Collection, [LC-DIG-det-4a19869].*

Founded by Daniel Henry Holmes in 1842 and moved to its Canal Street location in 1949, it was the largest department store in the South, with customers served by more than seven hundred employees. Meeting under the D.H. Holmes clock, located on the Canal Street façade, was a popular rendezvous point for decades.

Maison Blanche: The Finest Department Store in the South

Located at the corner of Canal and Dauphine Streets, the original Maison Blanche building was heralded as a palace by the *Daily Picayune*, which dubbed it "the finest department store in the South." The paper reported that the store was executed "with more daring and on a more superb scale than anything yet attempted in this city or in any Southern city." New Orleanians flocked to Maison Blanche for its opening day on October 30, 1897. The grand department store on Canal Street employed six hundred workers and had a selling space of 60,580 square feet, according to the *Daily Picayune*.

Locals grew up going to the Maison Blanche building for more than just retail shopping. The building was complete with doctor, dentist, attorney and accountant offices. The city's first radio station, WSMB, was founded in 1925 and made its home on the thirteenth floor.[55]

Maison Blanche and D.H. Holmes were eventually acquired by Dillard's department store. The Maison Blanche building is still in use as the Ritz-Carlton hotel, and the D.H. Holmes building is now the Hyatt French Quarter.[56]

Rubensteins:
The Most Exquisite Gentlemen's Store

Opened in 1924 as a haberdashery by Morris Rubenstein, a century later, Rubensteins is one of the most famed men's stores in the United States, renowned for impeccable service, custom tailoring and the best of personal shoppers. In the 1950s, the company expanded to six buildings stretching down an entire block of Canal and St. Charles.

From the beginning, Rubensteins was all about family. Owned and operated by the same family since its inception, on any given day, you can walk in and meet Andre, David and Kenny Rubenstein assisting customers on the sales floor. Rubensteins considers every single employee to be a part of that family, and it shows in the tenure of the team there.

Allison Marshall, daughter of David Rubenstein, initially never intended to go to work in the family business of men's clothing. She and sister Hillary initially opened their own women's store on Magazine Street. However, several years later, armed with a business degree and a desire to stay in New Orleans, she went to work at the store managing displays and advertising.[57]

Today, Rubensteins offers special services, including complimentary valet parking (the current valet has been with the company for thirty-six years), personal shopping appointments and free delivery. The store also offers expert alterations, made-to-measure suits, gift-wrapping, office or home appointments and a shoe shine and repair service while you wait.

An Interview with David Rubenstein

Q. Share the story of how Rubensteins came to be, the opening in 1924 and a little bit about Morris, Elkin and Sam.

A. Morris wanted to get married, and his future-in-laws said he needed a job in order to do so. Since there weren't many jobs during the early parts of the Depression, he opened the store so he could get married. His brothers, Elkin and Sam, soon joined him as the business grew. They chose to open a clothing store because clothes were important in those days, and they were young men who liked fashion. They had retail experience because their parents had a dry goods store at 618 South Rampart Street across from the Gem Saloon.

Q. Can you share a favorite story or two of working with Rubensteins clients?

A. We've got customers going back many generations, from people that shopped with us when they were young who are now shopping with their kids, grandkids and even great-grandkids. A lot of people bought their first suit at the Madison Shop, which was, in the early '60s, a mecca for shopping for college students. The Madison Shop was started by David and Andre Rubenstein as a young men's clothing store within Rubensteins. Now those same men come back as highly successful businessmen, living all over the country, and when they come to New Orleans, they come in and shop with us. It's also great to reconnect with old friends who grew up here and moved away or [who] went to university here and now have children going to Tulane. We have so many customers that travel in to bring their kids to Tulane and while in town come back to shop and bring their sons in to shop with them.

Q. Describe the general process you all go through when working with a client.

A. The first thing we do is talk about what occasion they are buying clothes for, and then of course, we want to know where they are from and where they live.

Q. What are some of Rubensteins accomplishments?

A. We've been around ninety years. We've had lots of people work for us who have gone on to many great careers—doctors, lawyers, politicians. We came back fifty-one days after Katrina, thanks in part to our great customers, employees and vendors. We are also extremely proud of all of the times we have read in books or seen in interviews [that former customers] remember buying their first suit from us. Some are highly successful and some aren't, but we made an impression on each of them.

Q. It's well known in New Orleans that Rubensteins has a track record of keeping employees for life. Talk about that.

A. We have one employee who has been with us fifty years, thirty-seven years and twenty-seven years. Lots of our employees retire with us—we're like a family and treat each other that way. Everyone works together and we all love being a part of it.

Q. Why do you all choose to live and work in New Orleans?

A. New Orleans has always been a fashionable city for men, and it's easy to introduce fashion to New Orleanians. We love the convenience of being able to live near work and all the great tourism business that brings us repeat friends from near and far.

Yvonne LaFleur:
A Destination for European Sensibility

A former clothing designer, LaFleur opened her eponymous shop in 1969. Trained at a Parisian atelier in the 1970s, LaFleur shares her deep knowledge of intricate tailoring with her in-house seamstresses. Complete with a bridal boutique, a fragrance department, an in-house millinery and a retail floor stocked with everything from gowns to sportswear, the ten-thousand-square-foot building is the epitome of high style and European sensibility. "Yvonne LaFleur is a brand," LaFleur told Missy Wilkinson, fashion editor of *Gambit Weekly*. "The store is built on collections I put together. If the customer buys something this year, the piece will evolve into something that can be updated next season, because everything is through one point of view."

LaFleur teaches her clients to develop a complete wardrobe by layering well-made classic pieces season after season. "The (shop) girls are trained in building peoples' wardrobes," she says. "A wardrobe we wear season after season is really about 10 go-to pieces."[58]

Hove Parfumer:
The Fragrance Aestheticians

Hove Parfumeur, known all around the world for stocking the best in fine fragrances, opened in the French Quarter in 1931. Alvin Hovey-King learned the science of blending from her Creole mother, and as the daughter of a cavalry officer and wife of a navy commander, she spent much of her life traveling the world. She moved her business to 723 Toulouse Street in 1938 and, in true French Quarter shop owner style, lived on the second floor until her passing in 1961. Like Rubensteins, Hove is a family business and has been passed from generation to generation. Hove is presently located in a historic building on Chartres Street.

Hattie Sparks: The Next Generation

Over the past ten years, the city has experienced quite an artistic rebirth: local designers are invigorating the classic New Orleans aesthetic as the garment industry rises to its former glory. For fashionistas looking to shop local and independent designers the destination is Hattie Sparks. In the Riverbend neighborhood, Hattie Sparks, owned by local gal about town Hattie Moll is chock-full of one-of-a-kind pieces and a charming selection of women's wear. Hattie is also quite the hostess. She regularly hosts in-store events, inviting fashion lovers from all over the city in for an experience that's much more that just shopping. She curates every component from the cocktails to the party favors, Hattie knows her customer and knows how to keep them coming back.

An Interview with Hattie Moll of Hattie Sparks

Q. Tell me a little about yourself. Where are you from? What's your educational background?

A. I am originally from Houston, Texas, and am the second in a family of six girls. We moved to Aspen, Colorado, when I was seven but traveled back and forth to Texas quite a bit. We finally moved back for good when I was sixteen to Kerrville, a town in the Hill Country about forty-five minutes west of San Antonio. I received an undergraduate degree in art history and business and moved to New Orleans immediately after graduating to pursue a master's degree in art history from Tulane University. I wrote my master's thesis on the Chicano exploration of identity, particularly in border regions, and framed the argument through the life and work of notable Chicano activist and artist Victor Ochoa.

Q. When did you realize you wanted to open a clothing boutique in New Orleans? Why did you choose the location/ neighborhood that you're in?

A. I had lived here for about three years when I noticed a shift beginning to take place in the city. People were not just moving back but were moving here for the first time, and there was all of a sudden this flood of new businesses. And people were really accepting and excited about this. However, much of this new business was food or beverage related, and new retail was lagging behind a bit. I recognized a gap in the boutique scene here—there was not much that bridged the gap between low end and high end. There also wasn't much that offered an all-encompassing experience or new, unheard-of or just-established brands. I knew I could do something really different aesthetically than what I was seeing, as well as capitalize on all the amazing design talent I was seeing pop up locally and regionally.

I chose the Maple Street neighborhood because I spent so much time over here in graduate school studying at coffee shops and just fell in love the with area. I was lucky enough to be around during a really transformative period for the neighborhood and got to watch some great businesses open and begin to thrive. It's really a local's secret gem of a neighborhood, and I appreciated the commitment that residents and businesses had to the area. I just felt like it was the perfect fit for a store like mine. Maple Street offers businesses the opportunity to really shine whereas on busier shopping stretches they might get lost in the shuffle. There's really something for everyone over here, and all the stores are unique but still complement each other so well.

Q. Describe the general process you go through to determine what merchandise you'll carry each season in your store.

A. Our biggest strength is carrying things that look very expensive and high end but aren't actually going to break the bank. So one of the things I really look for at market are pieces that have a luxe feel to them or special little elements that elevate the garment. I tend to shy away from "fast fashion," super trendy items because I want to carry things that women will wear year after year. If we do dip our toe into a trend, it's usually a subtle take on it. I read a ton of magazines and blogs and really try to take all of the images I see and use them to determine what it is that people might want to wear in the future and what they're actually wearing now. Obviously it's important to have your finger on the pulse of what's coming up in fashion, but it's equally as important to see what it is real women are wearing now.

Q. What local designers do you carry?

A. Jolie & Elizabeth, Camilyn Beth [based in Florida, made in New Orleans], EllenL Jewelry, Saint Claude jewelry, See Scout Sleep, Fit by You, the Grove Street Press, Lionheart Prints, Sarah Ott, Flying Fox, Krewe du Optic, Lipscape, Kismet, Loomed, the Elizabeth Chronicles.

Q. What makes your store unique?

A. We really provide an all-encompassing shopping experience and believe that there's something for everyone at Hattie Sparks. I'm committed to finding brands that have a unique element to them, whether it's the production process or the story behind how the company began. We have become a store where people know they can walk in and find things they won't get anywhere else in the city, and we are very proud of that.

Q. What do you believe makes a quality article of clothing?

A. Attention to details—whether it's the placement of a pocket, beading or how the pleats will fall on a skirt. Honestly, price has nothing to do with it. I've carried $75 dresses before that look, fit and feel better than a $250 dress. Oh, and fabric choice. That's huge. If the print is wrong or there's a weird panel of lace or it's scratchy—that immediately takes it down for me.

Q. Tell me about the girl who shops at Hattie Sparks.

A. She's a modern girl with classic sensibilities. She wants to subtly make a statement with her clothing but still be able to look polished and pulled together.

She's appreciative of the little details that makes something special and loves the experience of discovering something new.

Q. How would you define New Orleans fashion? And the style of the neighborhoods?

A. New Orleans fashion is so multifaceted and influenced by people's lifestyles and professions and is truly a series of complementary characterizations. It's old school but refined; it's thought-out but easygoing; it's colorful but polished; it's elegant but understated. It's really interesting to see how residents of certain neighborhoods have a pretty distinct style. The Bywater and Marigny are kind of bohemian and vintage; French Quarter is funkier, a little wilder. The Garden District and Uptown tend to have a more classic feel but lots of bright colors, patterns and different textures. Then you get into the University area, and it's all little cutoff shorts and lace crop tops, but then hop over to the Lakefront, where there's so much nautical and preppy inspired stuff. There's obviously a little of everything everywhere, but it's cool that we do have so many interesting little pockets of style here.

Q. Why do you choose to live and work here?

A. New Orleans lets you be who you are and doesn't ask questions. I've lived [in] a lot of different places, and it's the only place that I've felt like I was really encouraged to discover what made me unique. It's a city that, if you love it and really stick with it (because sometimes it's not the easiest place to live), will love you right back. Owning a business here is wonderful because the innate culture of New Orleans is to support [its] own and to back what's local and different. So hearing people tell me they'd rather shop with me than at a big chain store is always reassurance that this is right where I am supposed to be.

6

THE STYLE OF THE JAZZ ERA

There are only two things: love, all sorts of love, with pretty girls, and the music of New Orleans or Duke Ellington. Everything else ought to go, because everything else is ugly.

—Boris Vian

It seems difficult now, in the flood of music that fills the streets of New Orleans from Bourbon Street to Frenchmen Street and from the dive bars to the grand theaters that have recently relit Canal Street, to imagine that there could ever be a time when New Orleans and jazz weren't synonymous. While there are plenty of critics who will argue that jazz was founded almost simultaneously in a variety of places, there are others who will argue that the instrumental ensemble flowing out of the dance halls and brothels of New Orleans were uniquely their own and, therefore, a distinct musical genre.

"New Orleans Jazz," as opined by Al Rose and Edmond Souchon, editors of *New Orleans Jazz: A Family Album*, "is a product of the avenues and alleys of a unique city, polygot, multiracial, seething with love and conflict, a battleground of nations and cultures, a

An outing to the Jazz Museum at 1017 Dumaine Street, circa 1960s. *Louisiana Division/City Archives, New Orleans Public Library.*

landscape of mire and magnolias."[59] The musicians of the early 1900s drew from distinct sources: the minstrel show bands, ragtime, slow-drag blues, the marching bands, the vaudeville shows and classical sheet music. There's little question that New Orleans jazz began as a traditional music brought to America by African slaves and was played first in Congo Square.[60] New Orleans jazz music was perhaps the first American music and, without a doubt, is deeply rooted in the history of its players.

Mark Twain said it, and the jazz musicians knew it: "Clothes make the man." In the "entertainment" business in the 1900s, the Storyville girls knew one important thing, and so did the local musicians playing in the bars and brothels: first impressions were everything.

A full marching band plays into the night. *Louisiana Division/City Archives, New Orleans Public Library.*

Composer Louis Moreau Gottschalk grew up in the shadows of Congo Square and was an early groundbreaker of the New Orleans sound. His writing, inspired by songs learned from his white Haitian aristocratic mother, was unique.[61] In what is probably his most famous composition, Gottschalk employs an African instrument reinvented by blacks in America. He called the composition *The Banjo*. Gottschalk traveled and performed around the world; his attire was elegant and in line with the trend of the time. He wore three-piece suits, white ties, dress coats with the tails extending below his knees and a top hat.

After Gottschalk, the New Orleans sound continued to evolve. The specific sound of jazz is often attributed to Buddy Bolden.[62] Facts about Bolden's life are mythic. He was known for his loud, improvisational, ragtime style with a shot of blues integrated on brass instruments. He earned the nickname "King" Bolden, as he, with his powerful horn, was considered royalty of the dance halls and city parks. He had major influence on the jazz greats to come—King Oliver, Kid Ory and Louis Armstrong. Bolden's band was a nightlife fixture and quite the draw in the city of New Orleans for almost a decade.

Bolden was known to hang out at a friend's barbershop. The shops in Bolden's neighborhood served as social centers, just as shops in many African American neighborhoods are today. Bolden kept a crisp appearance—a tight haircut and expensive suits—and was often seen in the company of a woman, who would carry his horn. The few images that exist of the Bolden Band show the band all decked out in full suits, white shirts and bow ties as well. Bolden, considered a lost legend as he suffered from mental illness and alcoholism and died after twenty-plus years in an asylum,[63] was at least for a time, the undisputed king of New Orleans music and style.

Following Bolden, the new jazz style, the standard feature of the Storyville brothels, dance halls and honkytonks, was a sound of a growling horn imitating the human. Once, when taking a lesson from traditionalist Luis "Papa" Tio, the charismatic sax and clarinetist Sidney Bechet was scolded "No! No! No! We do not bark like a dog or meow like a cat!"[64]

Next on the scene, we have Jelly Roll Morton, who began his Storyville music career as a young teenager. His life was the stuff of legends. He credited himself as "the originator of jazz, stomps and blues," and while he was a master of tall tales, one thing is certain: he set a groundbreaking standard for the New Orleans jazz band with his *Red Hot Peppers* recordings. "There's nothing quite like it anywhere else," says Jim Cullum Jr. of the Happy Jazz Band and Jim Cullum Jazz Band. "The tunes and arrangements were all originals by Jelly Roll, meticulously created for the sessions. He hand-picked the top musicians on the scene and thoroughly rehearsed each number until he was satisfied. In those early days of the recording industry, this was very unusual—recording companies didn't give bandleaders the time and money for polished arrangements and paid rehearsals."[65]

"Depending on the whims of fate and fortune, Jelly Roll made his living as a pimp, a gambler, a fight promoter, a nightclub manager, a pool shark, a door-to-door patent medicine hawker, a bellhop, a tailor, and even a sharpshooter in a Wild West show. Jelly Roll Morton made hustling a fine art. When Lady Luck happened to smile his way, he sported a diamond gleaming in his front tooth, the finest threads on his back and a crisp

Fashion is architecture, it's a matter of proportions.
—Coco Chanel

Louis Armstrong and his band perform while being photographed by jazz aficionado Marks Grauman. *Louisiana Division/ City Archives, New Orleans Public Library.*

Edmond "Doc" Souchon and his jazz band are pictured in full performance attire—striped jackets and black ties—in 1967. *Louisiana Division/City Archives, New Orleans Public Library.*

Lars Edegran (left), a pianist, guitarist and arranger, chats with trumpeter and band leader Lionel Ferbos in the French Quarter, 1996. *Infrogmation of New Orleans via Wikimedia Commons.*

The Olympia Brass Band on tour playing on July 4. In the center is bandleader Harold Dejan, 1986. *Helmut Schmutz via Wikimedia Commons.*

The Dixieland jazz band the Louisiana 5, one of the first to record and tour, is photographed here in 1919. *Infrogmation of New Orleans via Flickr.*

thousand-dollar bill in his pocket. He carried a pair of pearl-handled pistols to complete his outfit."[66]

The list of jazz celebrities hailing from New Orleans is lengthy. A few other leading lights that certainly deserve mention follow.

Louis Armstrong

Armstrong, who has a park named after him on the edge of the French Quarter leading into the Faubourg Tremé, was one of the most technically sound jazz performers ever. His joyful and spontaneous energy in performance took him from coast to coast and around the world playing to crowds.[67]

Duke Ellington

The Duke brought a whole new level of refinement and elegance to jazz. A gifted pianist by training, Ellington's sophisticated arrangements as a composer allowed him to adapt and grow musically as styles changed throughout the decades.[68] Ellington most often donned an off-white dinner jacket in his stage performance. Despite the character James Bond getting credit for the trend, Ellington was the first to wear the style as a fashion statement. "The Duke really was truly an icon for the sense of grace and urban sophistication he possessed. His air of nonchalance and quiet virtuoso ability left the ladies in the audience swooned by his musical grace."[69]

Wynton Marsalis, the current artistic director of jazz at Lincoln Center, was born to a family of musicians and is an absolute powerhouse. He has won nine Grammy awards and a Pulitzer Prize for Music.[70] Marsalis shares his perspective of the music in the documentary film *Faubourg Tremé: The Untold Story of Black New Orleans*, explaining that, for him, jazz provided a form of expression and freedom that transcended the restrictions and inequalities of American society.[71] Marsalis's style is classically refined with a dash of confident brashness, just like his music.

Today, the city's most fashionable gentlemen attribute the jazz influence to the current trends and style of men's dressing. New Orleans writer L. Kasimu Harris says New Orleans men "definitely dress for [the] heat, and our attitude comes out as far as being easygoing and being really improvisational—the roots of jazz and black American music. With the advent of technology and prevalence of travel, a lot of people borrow from each other, so styles aren't as easily defined or recognized. But I think those three things are definitely incorporated in anything we do."[72]

When asked to define his own style, he said:

> *I came up in New Orleans playing jazz, where what you wore had to be as good as what you played; otherwise, it's disrespecting the bandstand. My dad always made me wear hats. Ever since third grade, it'd be cab driver hats, newsboy hats...But I'm a rule breaker. I compare it to music: it's based upon a set amount of changes. You wear*

a traditional two- or three-button blazer. That's the fundamentals, but then what I do with the blazer, the bow tie, the shirt I wear, throwing some sneakers in there—it's going off this path. I wouldn't wear wool with linen, but I will wear an ascot with shorts. People have been wearing bow ties for years, but it's how you interpret it to make your own unique personal style.[73]

The Jazz Funeral

The tradition evolved from a mix of European, Caribbean and African cultural influences and rituals. In nineteenth-century Europe, military bands were called on for all sorts of occasions, from commemorations to funeral processions, and in tribal West Africa, ceremonies for the deceased included music and offerings to the greater spirits.[74] In the twentieth century, African American churches, known for charismatic sermons and gospel music, coupled with the Haitian voodoo celebrations of life after death and the Mardi Gras Indian customs all influenced the current style of jazz funerals.[75]

A second line is in effect a civil rights demonstration. Literally, demonstrating the civil right of the community to assemble in the street for peaceful purposes. Or, more simply, demonstrating the civil right of the community to exist.
—Ned Sublette

While the jazz funeral has typically been for African American musicians, in more recent years, New Orleanians of all ethnicities, ages and backgrounds have been sent to the next life through this ritual.[76]

In the New Orleans Black community, death is commemorated as a public ritual (it's often an occasion for a street party). Every person is a son or daughter of someone, and every death should be mourned, every life celebrated.

—Jordan Flaherty,
Floodlines: Community and Resistance
from Katrina to the Jena Six

Flapper Fashions

The end of the war created an exuberant sense of freedom across the country. Spending was on the rise, the youth culture for the first time was dictating style and the dance halls and jazz sound, jubilant and rambunctious, spilled into the streets across the country.

Women won the right to vote in 1920, and that victory meant a "new woman" was on the scene. She

Opposite, top: The "first line" marching band leads a second line of a partygoers down Bourbon Street. *Photo by Jorge de la Torriente.*

Opposite, bottom: The march of a traditional jazz funeral. The marching band leads a processional celebrating the deceased being free of worldly pain. *Sheila Dion via Flickr.*

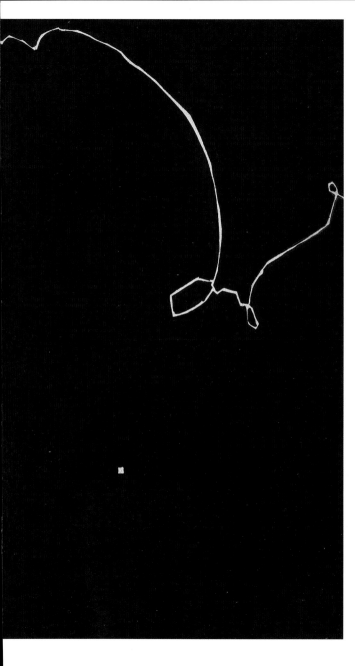

Where There's Smoke There's Fire by Russell Patterson shows a woman in an embellished drop-waist flapper dress, bracelets, a cigarette and a cropped bob hairstyle. *Library of Congress, Prints & Photographs Division, [r LC-DIG-ppmsca-01589].*

was educated and had a respectable job, at least until she landed a husband. She danced and partied all night, smoked and drank like the boys, wore makeup like the Storyville girls and was a risk taker like never before.

The Charleston, a total hit after debuting in a Broadway show featuring African American performers, was the most popular of the dance hall dances. Victorian-era garments, with their corsets, full sleeves and layers of crinolines, were cast aside. The new styles needed to be functional and movable as the girls were swinging, flipping and spinning on the dance floor. The women's apparel market spurred the growth of the first major fashion magazines—*Vogue*, the *Queen* and *Harper's Bazaar*. The advertising in the magazines targeted the new woman's independence and femininity.[77]

The term "flapper" came from the baby bird in the nest attempting to fly—an accurate description of the young and free girl revolting against the admonition of past society. In quite a reversal, the American girls became the trendsetters for the French. French publications glamorized the flapper style, depicting a new craze of exotic fashions on the dance floors of the hippest clubs. The girls were described as being "giddy, rouged and clipped, careening to the lewd strains of the jazz quartet."[78]

Their drop-waist dresses with loosely cut arms gave room through the hips and shoulders and were paired with beads inspired by the Coco Chanel pearls. Their dresses were rich in color with detailed ornamentation, sequins and imagery. Bangles and bracelets, reminiscent of the

African tribal women, jangled on their wrists when they danced.[79] The flapper hairstyle was a reflection of function as well; for practicality's sake, long hair was cut down into a streamlined bob. The girls often wore short-brimmed hats and turbans. The turban was inspired by the traditional people of Asia and Northern Africa who wore the turbans as "spiritually protective gear."[80] The American women wore turbans to signify their wild and free exoticism. In regards to footwear, because of the dancing craze, heels came down, and the cross-over strap and T-bar style helped to keep shoes in place. Pointy toes became popular as they accented the feet as they were kicked high on the dance floor.[81]

The flapper fashion styles were some of the first women's wear garments to be mass marketed. The reason? They fit women of any size, and the simple lines leant to ease of construction. Geometric patterns, prints and fringe reflected the improvisational aspect of the jazz music.

7

MARDI GRAS COSTUMES AND COUTURE

To encapsulate the notion of Mardi Gras as nothing more than a big drunk is to take the simple and stupid way out, and I, for one, am getting tired of staying stuck on simple and stupid.

Mardi Gras is not a parade. Mardi Gras is not girls flashing on French Quarter balconies. Mardi Gras is not an alcoholic binge.

Mardi Gras is bars and restaurants changing out all the CD's in their jukeboxes to Professor Longhair and the Neville Brothers, and it is annual front-porch crawfish boils hours before the parades so your stomach and attitude reach a state of grace, and it is returning to the same street corner, year after year, and standing next to the same people, year after year—people whose names you may or may not even know but you've watched their kids grow up in this public tableau and when they're not there, you wonder: Where are those guys this year?

It is dressing your dog in a stupid costume and cheering when the marching bands go crazy and clapping and saluting the military bands when they crisply snap to.

Now that part, more than ever.

It's mad piano professors converging on our city from all over the world and banging the 88s until dawn and laughing at the hairy-shouldered men in dresses too tight and stalking the Indians under Claiborne overpass and thrilling the years you find them and lamenting the years you don't and promising yourself you will next year.

It's wearing frightful color combinations in public and rolling your eyes at the guy in your office who—like clockwork, year after year—denies that he got the baby in the king cake and now someone else has to pony up the ten bucks for the next one.

Mardi Gras is the love of life. It is the harmonic convergence of our food, our music, our creativity, our eccentricity, our neighborhoods, and our joy of living. All at once.

—*Chris Rose*, 1 Dead in Attic:
Post-Katrina Stories

Carnival time in New Orleans—there is absolutely nothing like it on the planet.

It means full-on festivities: king cake, throws and parades and, of course, the Carnival costumes and

couture. But it's not just rowdy tourists and locals alike donning sequins and beads; the tradition goes much deeper, so let's take a look back at where the celebration began.

The French brought Mardi Gras to New Orleans; however, the origins of Mardi Gras go back way further than the French. One thought is that Carnival celebrations come from the lineage of the Roman festival of Lupercalia. Held in mid-February, it was intended to thwart pagan spirits and purify the people of the city. The ancient rituals correlate to those of

Opposite, top: Never an empty seat: packed bleachers and a crowded Carnival street as revelers await the parade. *Louisiana Division/ City Archives, New Orleans Public Library*

Opposite, bottom: The Pussyfooters, accompanied by a jazz band, dance along Bienville Street in the French Quarter during Carnival. *GW Fins via Flickr.*

Mardi Gras maskers postcard from the early 1900s. *Postcard published by J. Scordill.*

Carnival, created as a period of merriment that would serve as a prelude to the penitential season of Lent.[82]

Another theory is that the ancient rites can be traced to the festival of the winter solstice—Saturnia, memorializing the death and rebirth of nature, complete with a mock king, drinking, dancing, costumes and masks. Sounds similar, yes?

The Costumes

Mardi Gras became an official Christian holiday in 1582 in preparation for Lent with the idea that partying and foolery would be over when the time came to observe the obligations of Lent. Early European Carnival festivities allowed for the common people to "run wild in the streets—including mass inebriation, insubordination, and mockery at the expense of the ruling elites."[83]

The Greek god of wine, Dionysus, likely the unofficial patron god of Carnival, encouraged frenzied madness and costumed theatrics. Dionysus is the god of stepping outside of oneself to revel in the ecstasy of celebration.[84] The tradition of costumes likely originated then, as folks dressed as priests or nuns, impersonated nobles and danced about in parodies of religious rituals.

The first recorded account of masquerading for Carnival in New Orleans comes from the "Caillot

Left: An alligator costume design for the krewe of Comus, illustrated by Charles Briton. *Alligator*, print, 1873. *Infrogmation of New Orleans via Wikimedia Commons.*

Right: A zebra costume design for the krewe of Comus, illustrated by Charles Briton. *Zebra*, print, 1873. *Infrogmation of New Orleans via Wikimedia Commons.*

From *James Wells Champney,* The Carnival—"White and Black Join in Its Masquerading," *engraved illustration in Edward King* depicts an early Carnival street celebration. The Great South *(Hartford, CT: American Publishing Co., 1875), 38.*

Manuscript." Caillot, a Frenchman, came from the household of the dauphin, the son of King Louis XIV. He was accustomed to the regalest of celebrations back home, including ceremonial dress, masks, music and dancing. He wrote in his journal of proposing a Mardi Gras masking to his New World colleagues, who were missing the festivities of their French home. He fancied himself as the "most coquettishly" dressed member of his group as they road into Bayou St. John, he dressed as a "shepherdess, all in white complete with a corset, beauty marks, 'plumped up' breasts, and a muslin skirt."[85]

The Krewes

The first New Orleans Mardi Gras parade hit the streets as elaborately dressed partygoers, emulating parades they'd observed in Paris, and reveled through them in 1827. Thirty years later, the first recorded krewe was established.

The krewes, considered secret societies, are a New Orleans Carnival scene fixture. The members dress in highly detailed costumes, including masks, trinkets and beads, often times made by hand by the wearer. The krewe's queen and her court in couture gowns of crystal, lace and silk rosettes are honored at each krewe's Carnival ball.

A Mardi Gras masker aboard a parade float wears the full costume complete with feathers, sequins and beading. *Photo from William Metcalf Jr.*

As a French city, the Carnival balls and festivities were grand; however, under Spanish rule, the festivities were banned. One hundred years after the city's founding, the festivities once again flourished as the Creole population influenced the new American government. Carnival in New Orleans with the kaleidoscope of cultures became a multifaceted extravaganza incorporating old rituals and traditions with new rules and rites. "New Orleans, which is forever, unimpressed by reason or righteousness, and is mostly anti-modern, is the most Dionysean of American cities,"[86] opined art critic D. Eric Bookhardt in the *Gambit Weekly*.

A Mardi Gras maid on her Carnival parade float. *Louisiana Division/City Archives, New Orleans Public Library.*

Mayor de Lesseps S. Morrison presents Queen Ethel Elizabeth Seiler at the krewe of Hermes ball in the Municipal Auditorium, 1952. *Louisiana Division/City Archives, New Orleans Public Library.*

A group of New Orleanians who were members of the Cowbellians (a group that had presented New Year's Eve parades in Mobile since 1831), formed the first official New Orleans krewe of Comus. Comus actually coined the term *krewe* and established the early traditions of parades, masks and the tableau ball. Comus was a secret society, as were the krewes to come, and until 1992, most parading krewes were not open to public membership. The city council enacted an ordinance requiring the krewes to open their private membership directly before the '92 Carnival season, and in defiance, Comus canceled its parades in protest.

Mayor Vic Schiro with members of the krewe of Choctaw at their ball on January 18, 1964. *Louisiana Division/City Archives, New Orleans Public Library.*

Rex, Latin for "king," is one of the most celebrated parades on Fat Tuesday. The first Rex parade was organized by New Orleans businessmen in part to put on a spectacle in honor of the New Orleans visit of Grand Duke Alexei Alexandrovich of Russia and to bring tourists and business to New Orleans in the years after the American Civil War.

The king of Rex reigns as the king of Mardi Gras and is credited with choosing the official Carnival's colors—purple, gold and green—producing its flag and introducing its anthem, "If Ever I Cease to Love."

The popular krewe of Proteus debuted in 1882 with a glittering parade that saluted Egyptian mythology. The Jefferson City Buzzards, the grandfather of all marching clubs, was formed in 1890. The first black Mardi Gras

High-society ladies shop for Carnival season gowns. *Louisiana Division/City Archives, New Orleans Public Library.*

Regal opulence: the king in a gold train and the queen's silver, trimmed in ermine. Both royals and their pages are adorned with rhinestones, feathers and satin finery. *Infrogmation of New Orleans via Wikimedia Commons.*

organization, the Original Illinois Club, was launched in 1894. Two years later, Les Mysterieuses, Carnival's first female group, was founded.

One of the first and most beloved krewes to make its appearance in the twentieth century was Zulu.

Seven years before its incorporation in 1916, this black organization poked fun at Rex. The first Zulu king ruled with a banana stalk scepter and a lard-can crown. While Rex entered the city via a Mississippi River steamboat, Zulu used an oyster lugger to plow up the New Basin Canal. The city's favorite son, Louis Armstrong, returned home to ride as king of the Zulu parade in 1949.

Costume of traditional Zulu parade attire, photographed on Mardi Gras day. *Photo by William Metcalf Jr.*

The Zulu "Mr. Big Stuff" float—one of the most anticipated of the season with celebrity riders and thousands of coconut throws—rolls on Mardi Gras Day. *Photo from William Metcalf Jr.*

Perhaps the greatest change in Mardi Gras since the 1980s is the international sensationalism of the city's events. Conventions, which once avoided New Orleans at Mardi Gras, began using the merriment as a reason to visit. Camera crews and news reporters from Japan, Europe and Latin America travel in to showcase the festivities to their audiences back at home. Mardi Gras has become a full-time industry even in the off-season. Conventions and tourists now create their own version of mini-parades and balls all year round.[87]

The Mardi Gras Indians

So many of the Mardi Gras traditions are shrouded in mystery and secrets. Like the krewes, the Indians are a complex subculture with ancient and artistic practices dating to the 1600s. The tradition keeps alive the memory of a two-century bond between African Americans and Native Americans. The Mardi Gras Indians named themselves after the native Indians to pay them respect for their assistance in escaping the tyranny of slavery. The Wild Tchoupitoulas, the Yellow Pocahontas and the Wild

A Mardi Gras Indian in the traditional costume of feathers, beading and intricate embroidery. *Photo by William Metcalf Jr.*

Magnolias are some of the more famous "tribes" practicing today.

The Native Americans and the African slaves shared a reverence for the spirits of their ancestors and held a strong belief in the celebration of seasonal changes and the use of ritual costumes. It's a West African tradition of respect to dress like one's host at celebrations. The costumes of the modern-day Mardi Gras Indians are a blend between Africa ritual costumes and that of the Native Americans.

The first "Black Indian" costumes recorded in 1746 were made of turkey feathers and fish scales; they were worn by slaves celebrating Mardi Gras in their own way. A few decades later, the free men of color held Mardi Gras parties in costumes influenced by Caribbean, Native American and African cultures in the back areas of the cities and in the Maroon Camps. In 1781, the government established an ordinance prohibiting any persons of color from being masked, wearing feathers or attending night balls.

This early illustration of a Mardi Gras Indian Chief costume depicts the Plains Indian-style war bonnet, fringe and a peace pipe. *Louisiana Division/City Archives, New Orleans Public Library.*

Opposite: Modern-day Mardi Gras Indian costume photographed on Fat Tuesday. *Derek Bridges via Flickr.*

The reason? The masked revelers were often found sneaking in to the upper echelons' balls, which was absolutely not acceptable.[88]

The ordinance may have deterred the African Americans from sneaking into the balls, but it certainly didn't keep them from dressing in masks and costumes. The "Indian tribes" stuck to their own neighborhoods and Congo Square versus carousing in the main squares. As the tradition grew, so did the extravagance of the costumes.

The first Mardi Gras Indian suits included "Plains Indian–style war bonnets, consisting of a decorated headband with a single row of brown turkey feathers that descended to the ground as well as an apron adorned with beads, sequins, and other shiny items worn over a velvet or satin shirt and fringed pants."[89] The Indians gathered free turkey feathers from their neighborhood grocery stores; they cut beads and sequins from scrapped evening gowns and sewed decorative patterns out of everyday objects. The modern-day suits include intricately hand-beaded patches, which weave a dominant color and geometric patterns through the costume. Gemstones, ostrich plumes, sequins, ribbons and symbolic embroidery, including tribal flags and shields, complete the ensemble. The headpieces are ornate and worn over braided wigs and bandanas. Each costume can cost up to $50,000, and the more ornate the suit, the more prestigious it is.

Some suits are inspired by garments worn by the French courts and others include vèvè, a cosmological symbol associated with voodoo spirits.[90] The motifs often resemble the plaster ceiling medallions and other elements seen in New Orleans Creole architecture, suggesting a historical connection between Haitian and Louisiana Creole aesthetics. The process of designing the Indian suit is a true indigenous folk art.

In 1783, the Perseverance Benevolent & Mutual Aid Association was formed by free men of color to serve as a unique form of insurance and social aid to the African American community. This was the first of hundreds of such organizations and the foundation of the African American walking clubs and Carnival Organizations of present. As of 2014, there are about thirty-eight Mardi Gras Indian tribes; each tribe varies in size ranging from a half dozen members to several dozen.

Uptown and downtown each has its own group of Indians, one with West Indian roots and the other with African roots. The two groups of Indians, consequently, show their respective contempt for each other. In the early decades, the two groups would manifest this resentment in physical fights among themselves on the days of masking. There would be gunfights, stabbings and hatchet attacks as tribes would meet each other. In later decades, by the 1960s, the disdain finally gave way to a less physical way of resolving these conflicts. To be an Indian is a very special calling. It means defying seemingly overwhelming forces and making a stand for individual power. The method of resolution in current times is an unofficial contest of who can sew the most beautiful and elaborate costume. Today, the suit is the show, and the Indians wouldn't dare risk damaging their creations in any sort of scuffle.[91]

Today when two Mardi Gras Indian tribes parade by each other, it's a living theater of art and culture. "Massin' Indian is like a feeling that you have that you can't explain. It's a desire. An outsider wouldn't understand it. You want to do something that remembers the Indians."[92] "Massin'" is the slang for "masquerading," and according to Larry Bannock, who was the big chief of the Golden Star Hunters, "the only requirement of an Indian is that you gotta want to sew. This (tradition) is what keeps Mardi Gras going. People in the neighborhoods, the grass roots, working together, sewing and doing what they feel."[93]

Each tribe's dress is on display in a rambunctiously friendly competition of art, craftsmanship, confidence and style. Each Indian's suit represents hundreds upon hundreds of hours of effort by the Indian and his or her helpers and is generally worn for only one season and then deconstructed. The suits consist of specific parts: a vest covering the chest and back, a dickie around the neck, winged sleeves that open up when the arms are extended and an elaborate apron-type extension that hangs in the front and back. It's worth noting that while it's often called "masking," the Indians don't actually wear a mask. The garments are truly works of art and full of history and are appreciated by museums and historical societies around the world.

The Baby Dolls

The Baby Dolls originated at the time of the Storyville-era brothels in the unofficial and illegal Uptown red-light district. The first of them were the "Million Dollar" Baby Dolls. In response to Carnival celebrations happening in Storyville, the group redefined the New Orleans Mardi Gras tradition of marching societies. Calling themselves "baby dolls"—as that's what their pimps called them—they carried walking sticks to defend themselves while they danced in masks and costumes of baby doll dresses. Their costumes were made of satin, complete with stockings, garters and bonnets. The "raddy-walking (the name of their signature dance), shake-dancing, cigar-smoking, money-flinging" ladies strutted their way into a predominantly male establishment tossing dollar bills as "throws."[94]

As sex workers, these women were taboo, and African American women were certainly not considered "doll-like"; they smoked cigars, guzzled booze and were brash, raucous and provocative. However, their influence was so great "respectable" copycat groups popped up in neighborhoods all around the city as early as 1932.

Over time, the tradition of the Baby Dolls fell away; however, four years after Katrina, in 2009, dressed again in royal blue rompers with ruffles and bows, a new Baby Doll troupe danced along the parade routes to a new New Orleans style of music called "bounce." The new "Baby Doll Ladies" are reputable women with major talent and are headed up by New Orleans native Millisia White. White established the group with the intention of continuing the Baby Doll practice through dance and music.

In preparation for their first performance, White spent time with New Orleans elders to gain knowledge about the traditions of the original Baby Dolls. "When they saw us on the route...I kept hearing like, 'Here come the new baby dolls. The baby dolls are back,'" she said. "I could see in people's eyes for the first time...since Katrina, a glimpse of some kind of hope for a new New Orleans."[95]

Mardi Gras Couture:
The Tableaux Societies

Twelfth Night, the feast of Epiphany, was a fête of the early Creole society. Besides the feast, a series of balls throughout Carnival filled the holiday season

The dinner at the Atlanteans ball, 1940. *Louisiana Division/City Archives, New Orleans Public Library.*

wrapping with the final great ball of Mardi Gras night. The tradition was formalized with the organization of the Twelfth Night Revelers on January 6, 1870.[96]

The first balls included a preparty pageant in the streets, complete with floats (although much smaller than the grand-scale floats of current times), brass bands, torches and partygoers marching inside large papier-mâché costumes. The Twelfth Night ball of 1871 launched a custom that would become a lasting festival

New Orleans Twelfth Night Revelers Carnival invitation from 1884. *Infrogmation of New Orleans via Wikimedia Commons.*

tradition—the selection of a queen. A colossal Twelfth Night cake was cut and shared with all the unmarried young ladies in attendance, and whichever girl found the gold bean–shaped locket was then named queen.[97]

The Carnival balls were absolutely decadent. Grand hotels, theaters and halls such as the St. Louis Odd Fellows Hall, Werlein Hall, St. Charles Theater, Grunewald Hall, the Athenaeum, the Varieties Theatre

An early Mardi Gras tradition, the "Flambeaux" men light the streets for parade floats rolling behind them at night. Coins are thrown to them to repay them for doing so. *Louisiana Division/City Archives, New Orleans Public Library.*

The fashionable Carnival Queens of 1901. New Orleans Bee, *1827*.

and the French Opera House played host. Each ball incorporated a throne for the monarchs where the evening's court would be presented to the assembly and krewe members with pomp and splendor. The krewe would gift charming little favors crafted of sterling and enamel that included the date of the ball and the krewe's symbol or initials to the party attendees.[98]

The 1900s were truly the "Golden Age" of krewe societies; the organizations blossomed, and the parades and balls became more prolific. Despite World

War I and a devastating fire at the French Opera House putting a serious damper on Carnival celebrations for quite a few years, the revelers masqueraded in the streets anyway. In the middle of the century, growing international publicity and the attendance of actual royalty, including the Duke and Duchess of Windsor, reignited the extravagance of the balls and parades.[99]

Being a member of the royal courts requires lengthy advanced preparation. The queen and her maids have dress fittings with couturiers sometimes as far as a year in advance of the pageantry of the season. On the night of the balls, the attendees dress in their finest evening wear. Men of service dress in full uniform and the glittering royal procession dresses in elegant and extravagant garments fit for, and often with the price tag of, actual royalty.

So what's the process for designing a queen's gown? In New Orleans, the go-to resource is a Louisiana native, Suzanne Perron. Perron spent more than a decade in New York City on Fashion Avenue. Working for some of the highest-regarded design houses, including Carolina Herrera and Vera Wang, she earned her stripes—well, her crinoline and silk, actually—there and then returned home to open an atelier specializing in "once-in-a-lifetime gowns in white and ivory." Perron's approach is a collaborative one. She works one on one with the queen—from sketch to finished garment—and her goal is to create a gown unique to the queen's personality and style.

In March 2012, Perron released *Designing in Ivory & White: Suzanne Perron Gowns from the Inside Out*. In the book, she shares the process from foundations and crinolines, draping and patternmaking, pin tucking and folding and then hand sewing beads, lace, embroidery and hems. Perron, when asked why she chose to come home to New Orleans to open her studio, says she's committed to bringing something beautiful to the city of New Orleans. For Perron, it makes sense to make gowns of such distinction in a beautiful and historic city.

AN INTERVIEW WITH SUZANNE PERRON

Q. Tell me a little about yourself. Where are you from? What's your educational background?

A. I was born in Baton Rouge and lived in New Jersey, Delaware, Tennessee, West Monroe as a child. I have always called New Orleans home because the most consistent "home" in my life was my grandparents' house in New Orleans. My mom was born and raised here. My dad's family is from Ville Platte. No matter where we lived, we would spend summers and Christmas holidays in New Orleans at my grandparents' house. I even spent a lot of time sewing in my grandmother's sewing room. She would take me fabric shopping at Krauss's third floor, Promenade and Metairie Fabrics. I also loved to go to the Presbytere and Cabildo to see the gowns on display.

I graduated from LSU before completing a one-year accelerated fashion design program at the Fashion Institute of Technology. From there, I went to work for Carolina Herrera, Anna Sui and Vera Wang. I lived in NYC for almost fourteen years.

Q. When did you realize you wanted to become a fashion designer?

A. I started sewing at age five and, from that point on, wanted to design. I made my own clothes from age five on. I would wear elastic waist skirts that I made to kindergarten.

Q. Describe the general process you go through from idea to a finished garment.

A. There's four basic steps: consultation, sketching, muslin fitting, garment fitting.

Q. What are some of your accomplishments?

A. I won the Bill Blass Award for outstanding graduate in the one-year design program at FIT. LSU Young Alumnus of the Year 2007. *New Orleans* Magazine Top Female Achievers 2012, *Gambit* 40 under 40.

I was "discovered" by Carolina Herrera when she was the industry critique for my evening wear specialization class at FIT. From there, I went on to work for Anna Sui and Vera Wang. I also freelanced for Chado Ralph Rucci for many years.

Building a thriving business centered [on] my passion is a huge accomplishment—that and being a wife and mom of identical twin boys!

Q. Who or what do you look to for inspiration?

A. My clients are my greatest source of inspiration. I do find inspiration from some of the vintage gowns at the Louisiana State Museum. I am constantly looking for inspiration—from what I see people wearing, to Internet searches, etc.

Q. Share a favorite story or two of designing for a bride, deb or Mardi Gras client.

A. Oh goodness, I don't know where to start or narrow down. Once-in-a-lifetime gowns makes every gown I have made worthy of its own story.

Dressing the queens of Carnival is a dream I never knew I had. With my nearly fourteen years of Seventh Avenue experience, I am able to bring style and fashion to queens' gowns. Blending current fashion trends while keeping with traditions and expectations has been a challenge I have loved.

Q. What are your favorite fabrics to work with and why?

A. I do not have favorite fabric. All of the evening fabrics I work with have unique characteristics. Chiffon and tulle [are] great for soft draping. A rich silk satin can create a voluminous skirt. Organzas create ethereal volume. Beading can create patterns and spectacular light reflection.

Q. Why do you choose to live and work here?

A. Reason number one is family. Then there is food, culture, artistry, history... what a fabulous place to call home. If New Orleans were not the city where so much of my family lives and the place I call home, I would probably still be in NYC. The transition here was so easy. Creative professionals, a walking city, wonderful entertainment, great local retail and restaurants... so many parallels to NYC.

8
FESTIVAL FASHIONS

It was a thunderous afternoon when Joe Cocker took the Woodstock stage in a tie-dyed V-neck with his version of a skinny bootleg jean. The following morning, after Crosby, Stills and Nash & Young played through the night, Jimi Hendrix, in his now iconic fringe-tasseled cape, closed the weekend with "The Star-Spangled Banner."

At that same moment on the other side of the globe, Marisa Berenson was posing for *Vogue* in a Halston tie-dyed caftan. Yves Saint Laurent deemed her "the girl of the '70s." Berenson was one of Diana Vreeland's favorite models and granddaughter of designer Elsa Schiaparelli, one of the most prominent women in fashion and subject of the Metropolitan Museum of Art's Costume Institute exhibit "Schiaparelli and Prada: Impossible Conversations." Marisa was living a haute couture Parisian-American girl's dream. And in those moments, between acoustic set and electric guitar, through the lens of a high-fashion photographer's camera, the love child known as bohemian chic—or hippie couture and, more presently, festival fashion—was officially born.

While the rockers in New York were paving the way for one genre of music, the spirit in Congo Square circa 1970 was high as the city's first Jazz Fest lineup showed the world where America's richest music culture really lived. Mahalia Jackson and Duke Ellington led the Eureka Brass Band and a crowd of second-liners through the festival grounds, as the lineup in that first

Left: A dancing lady at Jazz Festival wears feather-detailed top hat. *Courtesy of Alicia Antoinette Photography.*

Opposite: A Mardi Gras Indian with a butterfly motif costume parades through the Jazz Festival Fairgrounds. *Courtesy of Alicia Antoinette Photography.*

A local, dressed in a cotton shirt with a piano motif at Jazz Festival, dances away the day. *Photo by William Metcalf Jr.*

Opposite: Jewelry designer Dourien Fletcher is dressed in puka shells and vibrant prints at Jazz Festival. *Courtesy of Alicia Antoinette Photography.*

year included the likes of Fats Domino, the Meters, the Preservation Hall Band, Pete Fountain, Clifton Chenier and daily parades by the Mardi Gras Indians.

Louisiana is home to over four hundred festivals every year, ranging from seafood and catfish to Creole tomato and strawberry. And that's just one end of the spectrum. At the other end, there's the blues, Cajun, jazz and voodoo festivals.

At the Fair Grounds Race Track, the current home to the New Orleans Jazz and Heritage Festival, festivalgoers make their way from stage to stage,

Seersucker trousers, a white cotton button down and a straw fedora keep this gentleman festival cool. *Courtesy of Alicia Antoinette Photography.*

through the crafts and the marketplace and past the Cajun duck po' boys and the boudin balls—stopping, of course, for crawfish bread and snoballs—in the distinct dress code that only those who understand the climate of the "northernmost Caribbean city" can follow. So while the grunge girl, hippie-rocker chic festival style is prevalent in other cities, in New Orleans, there's some marked differences in festival style.

In New Orleans, during fest season, the humidity is at its highest. New Orleans ladies know to let their natural beauty shine. Makeup is kept to a minimum, except of course for the Festival Queens, who require full regalia. Clothing must be designed for comfort: simple cotton, linens and lace, piled high with accessories. Rings and necklaces in natural materials from leathers to seed beads and puka shells can be purchased on festival grounds. Festivalgoers love color. The parading Mardi Gras Indians are an inspiration wearing monochromatic

A local gentleman, photographed on the Jazz Festival fairgrounds, keeps the sun out of his eyes and is all smiles through the heat of the day. *Courtesy of Alicia Antoinette Photography.*

and seriously vibrant hues. Often New Orleanians will add their most vivid bandana to keep the sweat out of their eyes or a wide brimmed hat while whirling around in bare feet. The weather in New Orleans can change in a moment, so packing an umbrella for either rain or the sun's hot rays is a necessity. Tribal prints are fully festival appropriate, and gentlemen at a festival know the easiest way to stay handsome in tropical weather is to pair a lightweight shirt in an even lighter color with loose-fitting khakis or seersucker.

9
LESSONS IN SOUTHERN DRESSING

Good clothes open all doors.
—Thomas Fuller

T he great thing about New Orleans, it requires you to
have parties," says writer and true southerner Julia
Reid in a conversation with the *Times Picayune*.[100] And
if there's one thing a good southerner knows, it's that
any fine party requires an equally fine outfit.

Southern belles, and gents for that matter, are
known for pulling off ladylike and lovely with a sense
of debonair dash. While fine dressing sounds easy
enough, in the New Orleans island climate, dressing
for the heat and humidity is a must. Somehow
the southern gals never seem to melt like
a wilted flower even in one-hundred-
degree summer weather.

Perhaps the most iconic southern
belle, Scarlett O'Hara, redefined our
view of women from the South with
her cunning good looks and coquettish
charm. And Scarlett certainly knew that
the most fashionable place to shop was
New Orleans. Shop owner Yvonne LaFleur,

*You can be gorgeous at
thirty, charming at forty and
irresistible the rest of your life.*
—Coco Chanel

Game time at the YMCA: the children are dressed for the weather, the staff are in traditional cotton uniform. *Louisiana Division/City Archives, New Orleans Public Library.*

Local children in cotton and lightweight fabrics take dance lessons at the YMCA. *Louisiana Division/City Archives, New Orleans Public Library.*

whose signature style hasn't changed in forty-plus years as a fixture of the New Orleans fashion scene reminds us: "Rhett brought Scarlett to New Orleans to shop. I like to feel this is where he would have brought her in a contemporary time."[101]

Before we get into the lessons of southern dressing, let's take a look at the "rules." Here's a few from the *Ladies' Book of Etiquette and Manuel of Politeness*, published in 1860:[102]

Mrs. Victor H. "Sunny" Schiro (right) and a friend wear the traditional white gloves and hats during Mexico Week 1965. *Louisiana Division/City Archives, New Orleans Public Library.*

In the summer a dress of light muslin is appropriate. White kid gloves, trimmed to match the dress, and white or black satin slippers, with silk stockings, must be worn.

In purchasing goods for the wardrobe, let each material be the best of its kind. To buy a poor, flimsy fabric merely because the price is low, is extravagance, not economy; still it's worse to buy articles because they are offered

cheap, when you have no use for them.

Never wear a dress which is out of place or out of season under the impression that "it will do for once," or "nobody will notice it."

Back in the 1860s, these rules were perhaps all a lady needed. In the days of Emily Post, the summer season fell between Memorial Day

Top: Traditional southern dress: she's in a breezy silk draped dress while the gentlemen wear traditional suits and ties. *Louisiana Division/City Archives, New Orleans Public Library.*

Left: A couple invoking a magic 8 ball at a party dressed in temperature-appropriate party clothes—a silk two-piece dress suit (her) and a short-sleeve button down with lightweight trousers (him). *Louisiana Division/City Archives, New Orleans Public Library.*

and Labor Day. Society folks flocked to the beaches and country homes to escape the heat of the city summers. Traditional city attire was packed up and left behind in exchange for lighter, and typically whiter, summer outfits. By the fall, with the return to the city, summer clothes went back in trunks, and more formal city clothes returned. It was an age when there was a dress code for practically every occasion, and the signal to mark the change between summer resort clothes and everyday city attire came from one's destination.

In New Orleans, there's lessons from Emily's time that still hold true. We'll start with lessons for the ladies first and then those for the gents.

Choose fabrics wisely. Lightweight fabrics in a neutral color are always chic and appropriate for daywear. Adding pops of color and details can dress up a simple cotton dress. On the hottest days, if the dress isn't made of cotton, make

Classic women's style, 1935: a linen jacket and a silk bow tied at the neck and a cropped haircut made popular by the jazz-age flapper style. *Infrogmation of New Orleans via Wikimedia Commons.*

sure it's fully lined. Minimizing the appearance of sweat is key. A sweet little dress allows for a breeze (something that pants are no good for) while being totally put together.

A young lady is
fashion forward i
a breezy lace m
dress paired with
sunglasses by loc
company Krewe
du Optic. *Photo*
Natalie Mancus

Opposite: A strik
young woman
plays racquetbo
at the park in tru
southern belle
fashion, wearing
dress belted at
waist with a larg
sailor-style collar
Louisiana Divisio
City Archives, Ne
Orleans Public
Library.

Dress shabbily they remember the dress, dress impeccably they remember the woman.
—Coco Chanel

Where should one use perfume? Wherever one wants to be kissed.
—Coco Chanel

A woman with good shoes is never ugly.
—Coco Chanel

Shorts can be questionable depending on the level of "dressed" up you're going for and are an absolutely no-no at several New Orleans restaurants. At Commander's Palace for Friday martini lunch, you won't be granted entrance unless you're fully dressed. Regarding hat etiquette, a southern gal knows how, when and where to wear a hat. Up until the turn of the century, a woman wouldn't consider going out without a hat. While that's changed quite a bit, the modern southerner knows that the only type of hat to wear is one that's made especially for her as a part of her full ensemble. Ball caps or menswear hats, unless attending a sporting event, are really a no-no.

In New Orleans, get an invite to the monthly Round Table Luncheon in the Fleur Di Lis Suite at the Royal Sonesta hotel hosted by the "dahling of New Orleans" Margarita Bergen, and you'll be fully surrounded by veils, flowers, feathers, ribbons and embroidery. A formal tea, luncheon or wedding is also the perfect time to wear a hat, and for the record, ladies can keep their hats on indoors.

New Orleans style is fully influenced by its French origins, so when in doubt, live by the rules of the original French style icon, Mademoiselle Coco Chanel. Much like her forward-thinking designs, the French style icon's prolific sayings inspire the way southern gals dress today.[103]

Now for the gents.

When in doubt, wear a suit and always wear it correctly. In regards to the jacket, the bottom button

Romantic glamour: beads, an ornate obi-style belt and angelic sleeves. *Louisiana Division/City Archives, New Orleans Public Library.*

The cast of *A Streetcar Named Desire* from a local New Orleans theater company poses on a streetcar. *Louisiana Division/ City Archives, New Orleans Public Library.*

Well-dressed gentlemen: full, turned up trousers fall at natural waist and ties that are short and wide, circa 1947. *Louisiana Division/City Archives, New Orleans Public Library.*

is never done. Follow this simple rules in regards to the buttons: "sometimes, always, never," meaning when it comes to a blazer, suit jacket, sports coat, double-breasted coat, vest, top coat or outerwear "sometimes" button the top button, "always" the second and "never" the third. The only time this doesn't apply is in a service uniform. The shoes should be

Gentlemen wearing the "Bold Look"—wide-shouldered three-button suits with broad lapels—at a New Orleans Pelicans game. *Louisiana Division/ City Archives, New Orleans Public Library.*

darker than the suit, and classics always work: navy suit + black shoes = golden. Regarding the shirt sleeve: one-eighth to one-quarter inch showing when arms are extended is perfect.

Regarding the pant break (where the pants fall on the shoes, creating a horizontal crease in the fabric across the front of the pant leg), the standard approach is to have a tailor adjust the length to hit midway between the top of the loafer. However, there's more modern approaches in today's suiting that work just as well. Pants are often narrower today than they were before. A full break is considered classic, timeless and a bit conservative, and on the contrary, no break or a negative break is quite fashion forward. The "high water" is now high fashion and is fairly custom in Italian suiting presently.[104]

Mayor deLesseps S. Morrison and local councilmen on a construction site in traditional southern menswear. *Louisiana Division/City Archives, New Orleans Public Library.*

At a men's outing at the golf course, participants wear breathable short-sleeve button downs and trousers. *Louisiana Division/City Archives, New Orleans Public Library.*

Men in suits and boys in T-shirts and short-sleeve button downs gather around a news microphone. *Louisiana Division/ City Archives, New Orleans Public Library.*

A well-dressed southern gentlemen knows that color counts. Metals should match, from jewelry to cufflinks to belt hardware. Colors and patterns should follow the seasons. Heavy fabrics like tweeds, although rarely necessary in the South and certainly not in New Orleans, are appropriate for fall and winter; neons and pastels and geometric and tribal patterns reminiscent of the Carnival costuming are perfect for spring and summer months.

Next we'll discuss fabrics of importance.

Men in traditional southern-style suits and hats attending a political rally. *Louisiana Division/ City Archives, New Orleans Public Library.*

Library

Seersucker

"Born out of necessity, built with pride" is the slogan of seersucker brand Haspel, founded by tailor Joseph Haspel Sr. in 1909 as a work-wear clothing line for laborers. The fabric, originating in the British West Indies, was one that Haspel felt confident would thrive in the southern market.

Today, the traditionally blue-and-white fabric has lived many lives. Often thought to be a noble fabric for the upper echelon, seersucker originated as a cheap American cotton version of a luxurious Indian silk. Fashioned into overalls for laborers and military uniforms for the U.S. Army, the name originates from the Persian words "shir o shekar,"

A stylish southern gentlemen, Sammy Bolds, visits the New Orleans library wearing suit pants of a light texture and rolled sleeves appropriate for the climate. *Louisiana Division/City Archives, New Orleans Public Library.*

meaning "milk and sugar," likening the texture of the stripes to that of the smooth surface of milk and bumpy texture of sugar.[105]

In the 1920s, stylish undergraduates from Princeton, in the spirit of "reverse snobbery,"[106] took up the fabric. The trend spread quickly through the Ivy League

Seersucker, a southern style staple, has been designed and produced locally since 1909. *Photo courtesy of Elizabeth Ray for Jolie & Elizabeth.*

universities, and seersucker became a fabric of the "true gentlemen."[107] Author Damon Runyon wrote in 1945 that his new fondness for wearing seersucker was "causing much confusion among my friends. They cannot decide whether I am broke or just setting a new vogue."[108]

The fabric, as of recent times, has made its way onto the runways of New York, Paris and Milan from the likes of European designers Jil Sander to Dries Van Noten, as well as American design star Marc Jacobs's eponymous line. It can be found in the closets of gentlemen far above the Mason-Dixon line. "Seersucker is a bit dandyish and Tom Wolfe–ish, which is a fun way to dress in the city," said Christian Vesper, a Manhattan executive.[109]

The seersucker suit was the first to be considered "wash and wear." Haspel himself staged quite a scene diving into the ocean in his suit during a business meeting and then wearing the same one, quite dashingly, that same evening to dinner.

Cotton

Cotton made an early economic impact on southern communities. Sharecropping (a practice in which free black farmers and landless white farmers worked on white-owned cotton plantations of the wealthy in return for a share of the profits) allowed for a vast labor force. While in the 1930s there were about two million cotton

model in a
ersucker and
otton dress by
lie & Elizabeth
photographed
the Historic
ew Orleans
ollection. These
brics are among
e most popular
r southern
essing. *Jared
ornsby for NOLA
ashion Week.*

> *Fashion changes but style endures.*
> —Coco Chanel

farms across America, employment in the industry was on the decline as machines began to replace laborers during the First and Second World Wars. Today, cotton remains a major export of the southern United States, and a majority of the world's annual cotton crop is of the long-staple American variety.[110]

Bensen's company has grown from a small entrepreneurial start-up company to quite the success story—helping an apparel factory double in size after Hurricane Katrina. At the close of 2012, as a three-year-old company, Bensen reported manufacturing over 4,600 dresses and put $350,000 back into our economy.[111]

An Interview with Jolie Bensen

Q. Describe the general process you go through to design from idea to a finished garment or collection.

A. Some start from a sketch; others start with fabric. We sketch, select fabric [and] then sew up a sample—it usually isn't perfect. Our factory manager then sews up a second sample from our original, to specific technical design measurements. We then cost it out with fabric and trim. If it's a strong style that we really believe in, and many boutiques place orders, then it goes into production, of which hundreds of the one style are manufactured. We find inspiration for dresses from just about everything—the older lady waiting for the streetcar that's dressed in a classic tweed jacket, the younger girls at music shows who throw on their favorite vintage dress. We dream up ideas for dresses, then sew them to life.

Q. What are some of your accomplishments as designers?

A. Our *Southern Living* layout is one of our favorites.

We're quite proud of our annual Junior Design Competition, in which we select, from hundreds of entries, one seersucker dress to add to our collection.

We're also about to reach a big goal of ours since we began—our 10,000th dress made right here in New Orleans.

Q. What makes your line unique?

A. We aim to design dresses both your boyfriend and grandmother will love—a classic style, that you can wear for years, not heavy on trends. We've seen women wearing our dresses from ages sixteen to seventy-six.

Q. What do you believe makes a quality article of clothing?

A. Lined, pockets, designed well. Maintains shape after several wears.

Q. Tell me about the girl who wears Jolie & Elizabeth.

A. She's the young, carefree girl who is fearless, brave and ready to take on the world; she's the twenty-something-year-old career woman who works hard and needs a dress as well made as she is; she's the beautiful strong mother who is dedicated to her family and deserves to look her best; she's the traditional, conservative mother of the bride who needs a dress that suits her appropriately.

Q. What is your favorite fabric to work with and why?

A. Seersucker—it's versatile, lightweight, breathes easy, which, in these hot summer months, is key to staying cool.

Q. How would you define New Orleans fashion? And the style of the neighborhoods?

A. New Orleans style is just as eclectic, creative and romantic as the city is. Uptown has a proper and pretty style, Downtown more serious, Mid-City is a truly blended community and the Marigny is a bit vintage and rugged.

Q. Why do you choose to live and work here?

A. New Orleans is a city that celebrates, encourages and actively supports its talents. From music to food, art and design, we are constantly inspired by how this city's talent is able to flourish.

Part III

NEW ORLEANS NEIGHBORHOOD STYLE

With nearly three hundred years of history, the style of the neighborhoods is quite a free-spirited blend of fabrics and textures and a vibrant vision. From the sartorial style and flawless fit of the professionals spotted in the Central Business District to the comfort without compromise of Uptown style and the romance and worldliness of the French Quarter, there's a unique blend of international history coupled with a modern aesthetic. The rising design stars building their businesses in New Orleans are creating a new fashion capital. The past ten years have witnessed artistic rebirth as the garment industry rises to its former glory.

A go-to resource for local designers is NOLA Sewn. NOLA Sewn is owned by Lisa Iacono, a designer and industry expert herself. Lisa was quoted in *Women's Wear Daily* (the authority for comprehensive business coverage in the world of fashion and retail) in regards to the apparel industry movement in New Orleans: "Garment making is still very much a living art and cultural pride here, more so than any other city I've lived [in]."

Lisa's facility includes a sewing room, office space for designer meetings, a salon for fittings and a fabric library, and includes seamstresses, a patternmaker and the equipment required to produce garments on a larger scale. Lisa's client list includes Camilyn Beth, Hazel & Florange, Loretta Jane and Libellule, to name a few.

An interview with Lisa Iacono

Q. Tell me a little about yourself. Where are you from? What's your educational background?

A. I was born and raised in Cincinnati, Ohio. When I decided I wanted to study in New York City, my father said I wasn't ready for that "den of iniquity." As heartbroken as I was at the time, it ended up being for the best. I studied fashion design at the University of Cincinnati's design college (DAAP), which is renowned for its co-op program. The co-ops allowed me to learn in on-the-job scenarios in cities all over the country. It forced me out of my shell, and I was able to learn about many different aspects of the trade.

Q. When did you realize you wanted to become a fashion designer? And then, how did you go from designing to deciding to open NOLA Sewn?

A. By around age twelve, I realized that fashion design was a viable career, and I decided that's what I would do with my life. Once I knew that was my goal, I applied it to every step of my path—electives in high school, college research and application, and I studied fashion sketching in any free time I had. My mom was really great. She bought me books about design history and how to put together an effective portfolio.

Upon graduating from DAAP, I took an assistant design position at Betsey Johnson and then eventually moved on to American Eagle. I loved my teams and New York, but something was missing in my heart. There was a disconnect between the reason I studied fashion design and my duties at work. I felt I could not relate to the customer I was designing for, and I'd lost touch with the craft.

In the spring of 2011, I quit my job and decided to take a hiatus from New York. Suzanne Perron offered me sewing work with her in New Orleans (I had co-opped with her in college). I moved into a temporary apartment in New Orleans and intended to work for six months while figuring out how to start my line in New York. Suzanne encouraged me to seek local factories. When I couldn't find one, I decided to start one myself, with the intention of getting through one season of production. I had no idea that other designers would start to pursue us as a manufacturing destination. When that happened, NOLA Sewn was born. And in a way, so was I. Now there is purpose in meaning in my work, and serving other designers is a gift. Every day is different, challenging and exciting. I feel like I'm able to utilize my brain and exert myself, and even though I'm not a totally functioning designer in a traditional sense, my role as a producer has fulfilled my life in ways I could have never predicted.

Q. Describe the general process you go through with a NOLA Sewn client from design idea to a finished garment.

A. The first step involves an intake meeting. The designer presents an idea to our team, and we pick their brain a bit to make sure we have a solid idea of his or her vision. From there, we create a pattern, sketch, tech-pack and prototype, which is fit and reviewed in depth with the designer. Any necessary or desired adjustments are noted, and we return to the pattern for updates. Then a new prototype is created and again reviewed with the designer. Generally, we are able to get a designer to their finished garment in two phases of this nature.

Q. Where do you look for inspiration when creating your own garments?

A. My inspiration comes from everywhere—movies, travel, people, music.

I like the challenge of taking an extreme concept, and applying it to something wearable and approachable. So a cartoon rainbow princess becomes a series of gemstone-printed dresses. A movie about cops versus drug lords becomes a very dark, shiny, textile-driven collection. Dreamy,

ethereal music inspires sheer, silk, liquid-esque eveningwear. I love the idea of branding yourself to a honed T. But I would feel very stifled if I couldn't ask a little diversity from my customer.

Q. What do you believe makes a quality article of clothing?

A. I believe great quality depends on a dual effort between designer and manufacturer. The designer must have an interest in their fabric. It doesn't matter how beautiful the design is—crap fabric will kill it dead. That doesn't mean it has to be expensive. It just requires time and energy to source the right materials. The manufacturer has got to take pride in three things: understanding their skill level and capitalizing on their strengths, using the appropriate equipment for the job, and meticulous quality control. This is just my opinion, based on my experience.

Q. How would you define New Orleans' apparel industry? Where do you seeing it going in the future?

A. I would define the New Orleans apparel industry as small, unique and very exciting. I would hope that with the amount of local interest in design and dressing, it would continue to grow in its own way. I don't imagine it's important to follow the model of another market city, like Dallas. I think it might be better to evolve organically and in accordance with the city's needs as they are presented.

Q. What's needed to continue to develop sustainable design businesses in New Orleans?

A. Money! Just kidding. Bravery. Because we don't have access to local wholesale resources, designers must have the courage to brave the markets in other cities, learn the process, fall on their face[s], get back up and try again. Mobility is essential for folks who want to approach their product in a cost-effective manner. If you can't get yourself to the fabric, it won't land in your lap on its own. And sales. Getting the product to market is essential for garnering the capital to produce that next season, if you're talking about a traditional design calendar. So yes, money. Development is expensive. Flops are expensive. And things don't always work out the first time. And that's OK! Raising the funds to continue to work out the kinks in your business plan is key to maintaining a presence in the game.

Q. Why do you choose to live and work here?

A. I choose to live and work here because it is the place I landed that allowed me to find joy in my career. I'm a believer in the idea that work is life, and if you don't like your work, you're spending 70 percent of your time doing something just to get to the weekend. And that's too depressing! So I am eternally grateful to New Orleans for giving me a place to find myself and my joy. It is my home.

The Neighborhoods

It's worth noting that in 1980, the New Orleans City Planning Commission divided the city into thirteen planning districts and seventy-two distinct neighborhoods.

While most of these assigned boundaries match with traditional local designations, some others differ from common neighborhood knowledge. The intention of the planning commission was to divide the city into sections for governmental planning and zoning purposes; however, some of the names that the city assigned are rarely heard outside that organization. There are pockets of uniqueness within each neighborhood, and we could go extraordinarily deep here. The photographs to follow, coupled with the brief descriptions of the neighborhoods, are intended to give a general overview of the special style this city holds.

10

CARROLLTON/RIVERBEND

Thirty-minute streetcar ride from Canal Street, in the farthest northwest corner of the city, the Riverbend begins where the streetcar curves from St. Charles Avenue onto South Carrollton Avenue. A tree-shaded neighborhood with spacious homes, the neighborhood has a college-town vibe. It's home to both Tulane

A family plays in the park among the Spanish moss and palm trees. *Louisiana Division/City Archives, New Orleans Public Library.*

Dressed in all purple, a favorite color of the city, a lady poses for an Easter tea party in a Riverbend backyard. *Infrogmation of New Orleans via Wikimedia Commons.*

and Loyola Universities and was originally a rural resort community outside New Orleans.[112]

Added to the National Register of Historic Places in 1987, the "official" Carrollton Historic District stretches south roughly from Earhart Boulevard to the Mississippi River and west from Broadway (officially Lowerline Street) to the parish line and includes Audubon Park.[113] Audubon Park features the Audubon Zoo, riding stables, tennis courts, a golf course and clubhouse, jogging trails, lagoons, baseball fields, soccer fields and more than three hundred acres of green space for people to enjoy. The neighborhood is presently home to university students and families and has diverse architecture, ranging from Colonial Revival homes to the typical

New Orleans–style "shotgun" to more Modern-style architecture the farther away from downtown you go.

Annexed in 1874, Carrollton was a place for New Orleanians to retreat from the hustle and bustle of the French Quarter and relax by the beauty of the Mississippi River. The retail stretch along Oak Street has grown and is known for the annual festival celebrating one of New Orleans' favorite foods, the po' boy.

The neighborhood also includes two fixtures of New Orleans nightlife that draw locals and tourists alike: the

Music played for the youth attending Tulane University's convocation, located in lower Carrollton, includes a traditional New Orleans brass band. *Photo via Tulane Public Relations.*

A double shotgun on Burthe Street near lower Carrollton represents the Riverbend neighborhood architecture. *Infrogmation of New Orleans via Wikimedia Commons.*

Maple Leaf for live music and Jacques-Imo's Café for delicious and creative interpretations of local cuisine. Nearby Maple Street is another popular destination for the college crowd, with bustling bars, bookshops and restaurants. From a shopping perspective, local boutique Hattie Sparks is one of the newest to join the neighborhood. Specializing in local and southern designers, the boutique joins the Adams Street area, which is home to quite a selection of locally owned boutiques.

The river winds its way around Carrollton, providing a perfect setting for hangouts with friends, picnics and family outings. Walk the levee from the Riverbend toward downtown on the other side of the zoo to find a popular spot for relaxing outdoors called the "Fly." The style of dress is casual and comfortable picnic attire and active wear, fitting of the students and families who call the neighborhood home.

At the annual Oak Street Po-Boy Festival, partygoers do the limbo under the famous bread, a city original from 1929. *Infrogmation of New Orleans via Wikimedia Commons.*

11

Uptown

To the typical Uptowner, New Orleans was Uptown.
—Margaret LeCorgne

Historically, Canal Street was known as the dividing line between "Uptown" and "Downtown" New Orleans and was for years the epitome of fashion in the city. The Uptown District, with its ancient oak trees, gabled Tudor mansions and Carpenter Gothic fantasies, begins upriver of the Garden District with the official boundaries of the federal Uptown New Orleans Historic District, listed on the National Register of Historic Places, being the river to South Claiborne Avenue and Jackson Avenue to Broadway.[114]

Uptown has become one of the most stylish neighbors in New Orleans. Encompassing about one-third of the city's area, it's a place where the sprawling homes are meticulously maintained and locally owned restaurants and shops give the feeling of visiting a village from another time and place.

Uptown was part of lands granted to Louisiana governor Jean-Baptiste LeMoyne, Sier de Bienville, in 1719. It was then divided into smaller plantations in 1723. The neighborhood includes Magazine Street, one of the

The Aldrich-Genella House is an Uptown home on Saint Charles Avenue that is on the National Register of Historic Places. *Photo by Jeffrey Beall.*

On Palmer Avenue between Saint Charles Avenue and Freret Street is this mansion, typical of the Uptown neighborhood. *Infrogmation of New Orleans via Wikimedia Commons.*

N.E. Sauls Grocery and Sandwich shop on Prytania Street advertised southern favorites "Luzianne Coffee and Tea" and "Coca-Cola" in 1936. *Library of Congress, Prints & Photographs Division, FSA/OWI Collection, [LC-USF342- 008219-A].*

Opposite: Garments from Louisiana native and Council of Fashion Designers of America's Designer of the Year winner Billy Reid are constructed with high-quality traditional fabrics. His shop on Magazine Street is a local favorite. *Photo by Hunter Holder.*

A look at ladies' dress shops on St. Charles Avenue, Uptown New Orleans shows lovely window dressing and intricate signs advertising the shop names. *Louisiana Division/City Archives, New Orleans Public Library.*

premier retail shopping districts in the United States that includes upward of 150 retailers. The street is two blocks away from St. Charles Avenue and is a haven for fashion lovers. Those searching for fine clothing or home goods, handcrafted items, used and new books, imported rugs, jewelry, ornate furniture or nineteenth- and early twentieth-century home furnishings head to Magazine Street to hunt for special finds.

The ateliers of local couturière Suzanne Perron, as well as young design stars Jolie Benson and Sarah Dewey of Jolie & Elizabeth, are located Uptown. The neighborhood is also home to some of the most well-known, locally owned retail shops in the city. The area includes the flagship location of local jeweler Mignon Faget; NOLA Couture, which specializes in ties with

Above: An Uptown girl wears a lightweight cotton maxi dress, perfect for the southern heat, and an oversized straw hat to keep the sun off her face. She stands near a traditional Uptown home. *Photo by Kaela Rodehorst Williams.*

Right: An Uptown lady strolls St. Charles Avenue in a seersucker dress after a fundraiser for the New Orleans Jazz Orchestra. *Photo by Kaela Rodehorst Williams.*

Local entrepreneur and artist Kendra Jones Morris is photographed in a traditional seersucker dress in the Uptown neighborhood. *Photo by Kaela Rodehorst Williams.*

Opposite: A professional young lady is dressed in white cotton for a southern summer workday. *Photo by Kaela Rodehorst Williams.*

Louisiana motifs, including snoballs, streetcars and fleur di lis; bridal and special occasion boutique and shoe store MIMI and Cece Shoe; and Perlis, established in 1939, catering to customers seeking classically well-made garments with a Cajun flair.

The area has always been home to a variety of ethnicities, including Italian, German and Irish immigrants, and a sizable African American population. Notable Uptowners have included jazz musicians Louis Armstrong, Buddy Bolden, George Brunies,

Harry Connick Jr., Percy Humphrey, the Neville Brothers, Joe "King" Oliver, Leon Roppolo; singers the Boswell sisters and Mahalia Jackson; author Anne Rice; inventor A. Baldwin Wood; ethnobotanist Mark Plotkin; professional football players Peyton Manning, Eli Manning and Drew Brees; and rappers B.G., Birdman, Soulja Slim and Lil Wayne.[115]

12

THE GARDEN DISTRICT

The Garden District is considered one of the best-preserved collections of historic Greek Revival and Italianate mansions in the country, including lavish gardens and scenery. The streets bare the names of the nine muses of Greek mythology. Dubbed the "Garden District" for its English-style gardens featuring lush azaleas, magnolias and camellias, this neighborhood is noted for its astounding scenery.

Official flags designating Mardi Gras royalty are a common sight throughout the Garden District streets during Carnival season. On the edge of the district sits the Irish Channel (riverside of Magazine from Jackson to Louisiana), home to Tracey's and Parasol's, two well known establishments famous for "beer, po-boys, friend pickles and of course, fanatical Irish good times." Locals and tourists alike dress in their finest on Fridays for Commander's Palace twenty-five-cent martini lunch.

Designed as an open system of interrelated parks, the district's many outdoor areas are home to locals bike riding with their children, walking their dogs or reading and relaxing in the grass. Magazine Street extends into

A polished ensemble with intricate texture and detail crea[tes] a perfect look for office to after hours on Magazine Stree[t] in the Lower Garden District neighborhood. *Photo by Kaela Rodehorst Willi[ams]*

the Garden District from Uptown and includes some of the more contemporary design studios and offbeat clothing stores and independently owned shops. Local favorites include Aidan Gill, named one of the best barbershops in the United States, and Funky Monkey, known for well-priced vintage goodies. The Lower Garden District along Magazine Street has been increasingly gentrified over the past few years, with new boutiques and bars catering to a younger, artistic crowd.

A gauzy cotton mini dress is worn by a girl on the go, photographed under the balconies of Magazine Street. *Photo by Kaela Rodehorst Williams.*

13

The French Quarter

There are few places on Earth where jazz musicians, strippers, priests, drunk out-of-towners, politicians, drag queens, and antiques dealers could all be neighbors, much less get along. The French Quarter houses them all.
—Southern Living *magazine*

Since the founding of the city, the French Quarter has been the hub. Perhaps because of this city's longtime acceptance of the diversity of its residence and the welcoming nature of tourists and newcomers, the pretension level is low. There's an air of anything goes in the French Quarter. Anybody and everybody is welcome to come as they are and dress how they please; and in the French Quarter, tourists and locals alike are found shopping the vast boutiques and galleries for wearable goods and art.

Today, people are drawn to the French Quarter for its Old World charm, the jazz on every street corner,

Opposite: This French Quarter girl dresses in a style that's both individualistic and retro in fashions from local boutique the Revival Outpost. *Photo by Natalie Mancuso.*

Staying dry in the French Quarter. The semitropical weather often calls for umbrellas and breathable clothing. Women wear their hair with natural texture due to the humidity. *Photo by Natalie Mancuso.*

Opposite: A street musician plays in the French Quarter for tips in a hat. *Library of Congress, Prints & Photographs Division, photograph by Carol M. Highsmith [LC-DIG-highsm- 11684].*

the French and Spanish architecture, fantastic people watching and the sights and sounds of the everyday celebrations. The neighborhood is home to street musicians and performers, budding bohemian artists

Dressed for the Southern Decadence Festival, a gay pride festival held each year in the French Quarter. *Infrogmation of New Orleans via Wikimedia Commons.*

and longtime high society residents. Residents are inspired by the architecture and the fashions of the decades and wear anything from casual, climate appropriate attire to costume-inspired ensembles.

Chelsea Darling, a local stylist interviewed by the *New York Times*, noted that in the evening hours, along the streets housing the numerous art galleries, the style lends to a more dapper, dressed-up approach. Darling also mentions the "shop local" philosophy of the

neighborhood. According to Darling, she and her fellow Vieux Carré residents buy local designer clothing and visit local boutiques to support their friends and neighbors.[116]

The Vieux Carré's independently owned boutiques are arguably some of the most eclectic, with a vast array of local designers and artisans represented. A few neighborhood favorites include Trashy Diva, which opened its first location in the French Quarter and has since expanded to seven New Orleans locations offering locally designed clothing, shoes, retro and pinup styles,

A man rides a bike fashioned for future floodwaters through the French Quarter shortly after Hurricanes Katrina and Rita. *Robert Kaufmann.*

lingerie, jewelry and accessories; Hemline, opened by a Brazilian couple on Chartres Street after finding success selling imported fashions in the French Market, now has sixteen locations across the South; Fleurty Girl, which carries the work of many local artists in addition to its own New Orleans–inspired line of T-shirts; Revival Outpost, one of the most well-curated vintage shops in the South; and Goorin Bros, a San Francisco–based hat company whose French Quarter success led to a second custom millinery shop Uptown. Another favorite shop sought out by locals and tourists alike is United Apparel Liquidators. UAL stocks high-end Italian and Parisian designers like Lanvin, Alaia and Martin Margiela with prices marked down by up to 90 percent of the usual retail price.

Some of the best regional shopping centers are also located throughout the neighborhood. The Shops at Canal Place includes upscale national chains Saks Fifth Avenue, Brooks Brothers, Tiffany & Co and Anthropologie. Directly next door is the Outlet Collection at Riverwalk, recently renovated and reopened, which includes a Neiman Marcus Last Call and a variety of high-end outlets.

On the southern end of the neighborhood, the French Market, a two-hundred-plus-year-old market, includes stalls packed full of tourist gifts, local art and fresh produce. Vintage and flea market fans can visit David's Found Objects, Greg's Antiques and Le Garage, all on Decatur Street, steps from the French Market.

14

Faubourg Tremé

*New Orleans, more than many places I know,
actually tangibly lives it culture, it's not just a residual
of life: it's a part of life.*

—Wendell Pierce

Named for Claude Tremé, a French milliner, the Tremé is a community in which black and white, free and enslaved, rich and poor cohabitated, collaborated and sometimes clashed to create much of what defines New Orleans's present-day culture. The Fabourg Tremé was home to Congo Square (now Armstrong Park), the southern civil rights movement, jazz music and one of the richest living cultures in America.[117] The neighborhood housed sculptors, bricklayers, writers, intellectuals, cigar makers and a variety of other artists and craftsmen.

"A century before the Harlem Renaissance and the modern Civil Rights Movement, Tremé was a center of black cultural and political ferment."[118] The oldest black-owned daily newspaper in the United States, the *Tribune*, an eloquent advocate for African Americans' civil rights, as well as *Les Cenelles*, the first anthology of black poetry in the country, were published in the

Notorial drawing of a house on St. Philip Street, between North Robertson and Claiborne, from 1893. *From* New Orleans Architecture Volume VI, Faubourg Treme and Bayou Road *by Roulhac Toledano and Mary Louise Christovith.*

Opposite: Notorial drawing of a home at Esplanade Avenue and North Derbigny, classic architecture in the Tremé neighborhood. *From* New Orleans Architecture Volume VI, Faubourg Treme and Bayou Road *by Roulhac Toledano and Mary Louise Christovith.*

This notorial drawing of buildings on Conti Street at the corner of Villiere depicts a neighborhood bakery, residential architecture and fashions of the time. *From New Orleans Architecture Volume VI, Faubourg Treme and Bayou Road by Roulhac Toledano and Mary Louise Christovith.*

Tremé in the mid-nineteenth century.[119] Because of the Tremé, New Orleans became the only city in the South with desegregated schools and an African American governor during the Reconstruction era. "When we look at the struggle for equality and freedom for African Americans, we have to look first at Tremé," says Brenda Marie Osbey, a poet and professor of African studies at Louisiana State University and Brown University who has written extensively on Tremé. "That's where it all started."[120]

The neighborhood was home to a prosperous and artistically flourishing community of free people of color. Often overshadowed by its sister next door, the French Quarter, the eight-square-block neighborhood filled with nineteenth-century Creole cottages and Spanish mansions is where so many traditions of New Orleans were truly born. "Our jazz idiom, the Creole tradition of political dissent, the craftsmanship behind our vernacular architecture—all had roots in Faubourg Tremé," says Lawrence N. Powell, professor of history at Tulane University and co-director of the Deep South Regional Humanities Center.[121]

Today, history is fully alive in the Tremé: the brass bands, second lines, jazz funerals and Mardi Gras Indians parade through the streets as they always have, creating a pulse and experience that can be found no where else. The style of the neighborhood, inspired by the early jazz days and the musicians who call it home, is the epitome of cool. Beloved jazz musician Kermit Ruffins has his own "speakeasy" in the neighborhood.

An elaborate headdress in monochromatic feathers and intricate beading is photographed during the Zulu parade on Mardi Gras morning. *Photo by William Metcalf Jr.*

It's a bit like an old-school supper club and in true-to-style fashion, Kermit's speakeasy has strong drinks, a quiet exterior and no website.[122]

Ruffins's signature style is a fedora or newsboy cap with a bandana tucked underneath; he often dons a suit or jacket and tie. Inside the speakeasy, it's often standing room only, and the patrons dress for a night of dancing. On any given evening, tourists and locals can be seen dressed for the theater as the Mahalia Jackson and the newly renovated Saenger are home to world-class acts, reviving the long-storied tradition of theater in New Orleans.[123]

15

Faubourg Marigny and the Bywater

There's an unexplainable magic here which I don't
bother trying to intellectualize
—Solange Knowles

Immediately downriver of the Quarter, a live music destination—from the jazz club–lined Frenchman Street to the performance art and gypsy street bands peppering the Bywater—as well as a thriving artist-friendly neighborhood home to a punk-style arts district along St. Claude Avenue, the Marigny and Bywater neighborhoods have a subculture uniquely their own. Solange Knowles, the hip little sister of Beyoncé and owner of a New Orleans boutique, is famous in her own right for her unique sense of casual meets effortlessly cool style, and because of the "magic," she's become a resident of what many consider to be the trendiest neighborhood in the city.[124]

The neighborhoods were, until recently, considered two of the most unique and well-kept secrets of New Orleans. The Faubourg Marigny, which was once the plantation of a Creole-born vivant who made the dice game "craps" popular in America and who dazzled

These hip Marigny girls are dressed in whimsical current and vintage fashions. *Photo by Akasha Rabut.*

New Orleans by his flair and enormous inheritance,[125] and the Bywater, named for its postal code, are often likened to the Brooklyn neighborhoods of New York. The neighborhoods combine old-school New Orleans with a bohemian and considerably hip culture.

Street art is a fixture of the Bywater, as is the edgier and eclectic style of dress. *Photo by Kaela Rodehorst Williams.*

As prices rose in the 1990s in the French Quarter, young artists and entrepreneurs began moving into the neighborhoods, and as of recent years, the style and happenings have been documented by *Vogue* ("The Big (Speak) Easy: Secret New Orleans Spots to Uncover"), the *New York Times* fashion/style magazine *T*, *Garden & Gun* and *Food & Wine*, just to name a few. The neighborhood is packed with some of the coolest hangs in the city, ranging from hipster dives to trendy design-forward spaces. Local favorites are often packed with the city's trendsetters and tourist looking for off-the-beaten-path fun. The list of the neighborhoods' favorites spots

A street-view snapshot of a house on Pauger Street in the Faubourg Marigny. The street is named after the city's first engineer and cartographer, Adrien Pauger, who designed the streets of the Vieux Carré. *Library of Congress, Prints & Photographs Division, HABS [or HAER or HALS], [HABS LA,36-NEWOR,77E—2].*

Opposite: The Caribbean color palate of the Bywater neighborhood influences the style of dress. *Photo by Natalie Mancuso.*

include Vaughan's Lounge, the Bywater's most famous music venue; Mimi's in the Marigny, a restaurant turned dance hall as the night goes on; the AllWays Lounge, a burlesque club with a rowdy audience; the cozy Apple

A model wearing
a vintage-inspired
cotton housedress
by Hazel & Florange.
The brand based
in the Bywater
neighborhood is
inspired by homespun
Louisiana fashions.
Photo by Tate Tullier.

Opposite: Frady's
One Stop Food
Stop in the Bywater
is home to po'boys,
muffalettas and a
regular crowd of
neighborhood locals.
*Photo by Tate Tullier
for Hazel & Florange*

Barrel, which has live jazz every single night; Bacchanal Wines, a let-your-hair-down joint that can be a daylong experience and includes a worldly menu, a backyard-style stage set-up and a wine bar; Blue Nile and d.b.a., groovy clubs in the "music district" of Frenchman Street; Hi Ho Lounge and Siberia, two oldie underground alternative venues; and the list could go on and on. Within the last few years, new restaurants with fantastic chefs and clean lines have popped up, including Maurepas Foods, Booty's, Oxalis and Mariza.

The Marigny/Bywater's hipster cred is actually long term: Jack Kerouac jumped off the cross-country train here in the '40s to visit New Orleans.[126] Today, Creole and Classic Revival cottages that stood abandoned after residents left for the suburbs in the 1950s have been restored. Historic banks, corner stores and even bakeries have been refurbished as homes and guesthouses while riverfront warehouses now accommodate artists' studios and performance spaces.

Weekends bring shoppers to arts markets, independent galleries, artisan shops and junk stores. There's a funky style and harmony that create a good time, if an admittedly weird experience for all. As of recent years, more and more outsiders are moving from all over the country into these two neighborhoods. "The storm put New Orleans on the map in a new way: the romantics kept thinking about it," says one recently transplanted writer living in the neighborhood.[127]

16

Mid-City, Bayou St. John and City Park

Your darling streets are filled with beautiful architecture, bright colors, gorgeous florals and the wondrous smell of jasmine and the occasional crawfish boil.
—Dominique Ellis in "A Love Letter to Bayou St. John"

C anal Street running out of the Central Business District heads straight up to Carrollton Avenue, directly through the middle of the Mid-City neighborhood. The neighborhood is home to cemeteries, the fairgrounds, breweries, rows upon rows of quiet homes and, of course, City Park. The park, a 1,300-acre urban green space, 50 percent larger than Central Park in New York City,[128] includes a botanical garden, amusement park and the New Orleans Museum of Art and is home to the Voodoo Music Festival, the City Park Golf Courses, several stadiums and bike and boat rentals.

Bayou St. John, sitting directly across from City Park, is a quaint community for locals of all ages seeking a bit more privacy in their day-to-day living. The Bayou, which extended much farther in colonial times than it does today, is a picturesque bit of water with small

A heart is painted over this X mark of the post-Katrina search-and-rescue team on a small shotgun home on Bayou St. John in Mid-City *Infrogmation of New Orleans via Wikimedia Commo*

Opposite, top: The entrance to the Greenwood Cemetery in Mid-City is photographed wit the fireman and el monuments in view shining in the sun. *Photo by Nam Vu.*

Opposite, bottom A classic residenti double shotgun-style home feature Italianate, Eastlake and Neoclassical Revival architectu in Mid-City on Jefferson Davis Parkway. *Infrogmat of New Orleans vi Wikimedia Commo*

Roller-skating at City Park under the palms wearing traditional daywear attire. It's possible the girls on either side are wearing school clothing or perhaps just dressed alike for the outing. *Louisiana Division/City Archives, New Orleans Public Library.*

earthen levees on either side. The style of the Mid-City neighborhood is relaxed and informal. With its residents spending quite a bit of their free time outdoors enjoying all the neighborhood has to offer, there's a feeling of easy comfort and playful energy. Tropical pastels and vivid shades influenced by the outdoors and perpetually sunny weather are an influence as well.

In recent years, quite a few local designers and creatives have begun to call the area home. One such designer is Amanda deLeon, who has shown her clothing in both New Orleans and New York Fashion Weeks. New Orleans' influence can be felt in everything Amanda does.

City Park in Mid-City is a 1,300-acre urban public park lined with benches and the classic oaks, photographed here in the late eighteenth century. *Library of Congress Prints & Photographs Division.*

From the look
book of Mid-C
based designe
Amanda deLed
a model wears
garment shown
at New York
Fashion Week v
a custom print
of the famous
Greenwood
cemetery and
cross embosse
on the front bib
Photo courtesy
Amanda deLed

An interview with Amanda deLeon

Q. Tell me a little about yourself. Where are you from? What's your educational background?

A. I'm from a very small town in North Louisiana. I studied architecture and interior design at Louisiana Tech. I never thought about being a fashion designer until I was several years out of college.

Q. When did you realize you wanted to become a fashion designer?

A. I've always designed and created my own clothing, but until I was asked to make a custom piece for a friend of a friend, becoming a fashion designer never crossed my mind.

Q. Describe the general process you go through to design from idea to a finished garment or collection.

A. There are so many steps between idea and finished garment. First, I create a first-draft pattern, cut it out, sew it up, mark it up, take it apart, change the pattern. Some patterns, like my blazer, uses over eighty cut pieces. It takes from two to ten times of me repeating these steps to create the perfect pattern (I've never had a perfect first run). Then, once my final pattern is finished, I sew a mock up in a similar fabric to the final piece to make sure all drapes correctly and the fabric is appropriate. Once all of this is decided, I create my sample garment. This includes all of the closures, interfacing, padding, lining and inner lining. After all of this, I send my pattern of to a grader for sizing. When I get my patterns back from the grader, I test each size to make sure they are correct. In some cases, I also have my patterns digitized to make it easier to create my printed pieces.

Once I have my samples, I go though them to weed out what I feel is filler or may not work with the particular collection. I have cut out up to twelve pieces and/or looks for a collection. You have to be brutal if you want your vision to stand strong. Just because you have it, doesn't mean you should use it.

When I design, there are so many different ways that I get my end results. I could sketch something and [have] it mean one thing then, but it could look totally different to me in a week, month [or] year. My most productive way of creating a collection starts with a feeling, an attitude about the day or my life in general. I tend to be extremely emotional with my creative process. It's not directly what is visually cohesive, but when I begin to play this dramatic idea, in my head, things just start to come together.

There is a lot of symbolism in my designs. Sometimes it's right in your face; sometimes it goes unnoticed. But sometimes I like having something that is just for me—that little secret that no one can take away.

Q. How do art, music and design support one another? Where do you look for inspiration?

A. Music has always played a huge role in my creative process. I listen to music that conveys my emotions and state of mind at that time. I don't force music to change my perception; I let it tell me my own story—how it relates to my life and what I think my life to be. My Fall 2014 "La-Nouvelle Orleans" collection began with the song "At the Foot of Canal Street" by John Boutté and Paul Sanchez. It wasn't so much about the song as it was the story told by Paul Sanchez the night I watched one of his performances at Chickie Wah Wah. I related to the story and how it was something that I grew up experiencing in the church. In the end, the collection was created as a guideline of what I would like people to wear to my own funeral. It is my way of having control beyond this life.

For so many reasons, art is another inspiration of mine. I believe that fashion can be art and vice versa. My work is a way of releasing my innermost feelings to the world of fashion. I often wonder why fashion is my chosen field, but it is just what I do. Maybe it's because I fell into it, maybe because I like engineering and creating structure out of fabric or maybe it's just the beginnings of what I am to accomplish. I do know that no matter what I do, it will be of great quality and meaning.

Q. What do you believe makes a quality article of clothing?

A. Creating quality is not an easy task. It has taken me years of learning from my drafting skills to create the proper fit and shape. Fit, materials, construction and design are all aspects that make for a quality piece. I believe the person [who] wears my brand is someone [who] collects articles of clothing that will stand the test of time, that are classic in fit and shape, but want something interesting, something special. She is not concerned with what others are wearing because she is an individual [who] places great value on her own personal style.

Q. What are your favorite fabrics to work with and why?

A. I've worked with many different materials, but my favorite has to be leather. Leather is incredibly versatile, and I continue to find new and inventive ways of making it work for my ideas.

Q. How would you define New Orleans's fashion? And the style of the neighborhoods?

A. I think New Orleans is eccentric— eccentric in fashion, ideas and character. She is not a trend, but a collector of all things strange and beautiful. I don't feel that neighborhoods in New Orleans have enough personal style to characterize them as special or different. Of course, there is the Uptown versus downtown (in this case, the Bywater). But, it's no different than saying that the Upper East Side of Manhattan is different than Brooklyn.

Q. Why do you choose to live and work here?

A. I have chosen New Orleans to be the place I live and work for several reasons. I'm close to family, it gives me the creativity that I crave in my surroundings and people here are incredibly friendly. People here allow you to be who you are. This isn't to say that I would change who I am to appease the masses, but it does come without any pressure here in New Orleans.

17

THE WAREHOUSE AND ARTS DISTRICT AND THE CBD

A ride on a St. Charles streetcar will take a visitor away from the exotic French Quarter and directly into a business district similar to what one would find in the standard downtowns of America. The neighborhood is home to city's revitalized Arts District. The area, originally an industrial

A view up the 100 and 200 blocks of Saint Charles Avenue from the start of the nineteenth century. *Beinecke Rare Book & Manuscript Library, Yale University.*

Fashion designer Matthew Arthur, a Ne Orleans local and *Project Runway* star, wears a timeless style a classic suit and bc tie. Photographed ir the Central Business Disrict. *Photo by Natalie Mancuso.*

Opposite: Dressed i a cheerful cotton flc dress with a snoball in hand, this young woman exemplifies a typical summer weekend in the Cen Business District. *Pho by Natalie Mancusc*

A typical hustling and bustling workday crowd on Canal Street in the Central Business District of New Orleans. *Louisiana Division/ City Archives, New Orleans Public Library.*

neighborhood, was transformed in 1976 with the opening of the Contemporary Arts Center. The CAC is a ten-thousand-square-foot space home to music, theater, dance and arts of all kinds. The opening of the CAC led to the creation of a district that's become known as "the SoHo of the South."[129]

Art lovers can visit any of the twenty-five-plus galleries that call the area home, and today, business professionals, tourists and convention attendees are spotted all around the neighborhood at the many award-winning restaurants and music venues. The style of the neighborhood is one of dressed-up elegance. The charm and warm hospitality abound, and while the attire is a bit more buttoned up, the culture of creative collaboration still permeates through the styles that the locals are wearing.

IN CLOSING

Leaving New Orleans also frightened me considerably. Outside of the city limits the heart of darkness, the true wasteland begins.
—John Kennedy Toole, A Confederacy of Dunces

New Orleans is a living and breathing culture full of much spirit and history. From the very beginning, it has been a city of vibrant dreams, full of quirky creativeness everywhere. Whether it's street art or jazz music, there's inspiration everywhere. Its uniquely colorful flair for life is felt on every corner. The young entrepreneurs and creatives and the longtime residents blend brilliantly to share old and new forms of life, art, music, food and fashion. The people of the city, both old and new, are driven to create a sustainable future for the city they love so much. We'll close with an interview with Justin Shiels, one of the city's noted rising stars and an advocate for creative industry across the South.

An Interview with Justin Shiels, Founder of INVADE

Q. Tell me a little about yourself. Where are you from? What's your educational background?

A. I'm originally from Memphis and moved to New Orleans, sight unseen, for undergrad at Loyola University. I think I started as business major, then switched to visual arts and finally settled on graphic design. Thinking about it, though, I think all three are distinct paths that correlate with where I ended up.

Currently I am the publisher and creative director for INVADE, a creative culture lifestyle brand that specializes in a weekly e-mail, a beautiful quarterly print magazine and in-person events and workshops.

I also run a boutique design studio called This Creative Lab.

Q. When did you realize you wanted to work in creative industries?

A. I think creativity is in my DNA. My sister taught me to draw when I was very young, and I designed everyone's campaign posters for class elections. I even ran an e-zine in the AOL days. So I think it just was natural, to get my first job as a graphic and web designer right out of school.

Q. Tell me about INVADE, from initial concept to what it has become today.

A. INVADE has always been about the power of local creative culture. I started the site in 2009 and specifically focused on New Orleans fashion, music and culture. As we've grown and developed, I think my goals and passions have changed.

My goal now is to change the way the world sees the South. We are the next creative mecca, and I want to be a significant part of developing that narrative.

Q. Describe the general process you go through when creating.

A. My creative process always starts with brainstorming and research. I like all of my decisions to be grounded in thoughtful exploration.

I also really like to set specific time frames for working and editing. Usually to get a few ideas out of my head, I'll give myself forty-five minutes to start a design or article. Then I'll take a break and later give myself forty-five minutes to make edits.

The hardest parts about being a creative is simply starting. There is something daunting about a blank page.

The second-hardest part is giving your brain time to work out the problems. Editing is almost always the key to great work.

Q. How do art, music and design support one another?

A. Art, music and design are so interconnected. The perfect playlist will fuel an amazing design and taking a break to see an art show will bring me the inspiration for future projects. I also think fashion falls into that equation. I don't put much thought into my day-to-day wear, but when I'm going to an event or throwing a launch party, I go through a full process to curate a look that tells a story.

Q. Where do you look for inspiration?

A. One of the great things about goINVADE.com is that I have a finger on the pulse of local creative culture. I find my inspiration from the great makers, thinkers and doers in my community.

Q. What do you see for the future of creative industries in New Orleans and across the South?

A. I grew up in the '90s, probably the pinnacle of mainstream media. We knew what was cool because we saw it on MTV. But the Internet has broken down those walls. Audiences are fragmented, and anyone can find their own hyper-specific niche online.

When I look at the creative industries, I see a beautiful moment where independent makers can build a sustainable living by creating their own products. While there's still power in mass marketability, it's not completely necessary.

Q. How would you define New Orleans's fashion industry? Where do you seeing it going in future?

A. New Orleans fashion is so much more than seersucker and big hats. I'm proud to see a movement of independent creatives carving their own path[s] in a vast array of materials and styles. It just shows that the South has outgrown those stereotypes. This vibrant community is a force to be reckoned with.

Q. What's needed to continue to develop sustainable businesses in New Orleans?

A. Since the beginning of time, artists have always relied heavily on patronage. I think that's the secret ingredient that we're missing in New Orleans. We need more people with deep pockets to believe in this creative movement.

I think it's happening, but I do wish it would happen a little faster.

Q. Why do you choose to live and work here?

A. Living in New Orleans for the past eleven years has molded me as an artist and entrepreneur. There is a magic to this city that makes you fall in love. I'm thankful for it and I'm inspired by it.

NOTES

Preface

1. Quotation by Alan Jaffe, founder of Preservation Hall.

Part I

2. Sharon Keating, "Haunted in New Orleans: St. Louis Cathedral Hauntings," Go New Orleans, http://goneworleans.about.com (accessed February 2014).
3. John Garvey and Mary Lou Widmer, *Beautiful Crescent: A History of New Orleans* (Reserve, LA: Garmer Press, Incorporated, 2012).
4. United States Geological Survey.
5. Philip Kearey and Frederick J. Vine, *Global Tectonics, Blackwell Science*, 2nd ed. (West Sussex, UK: Wiley-Blackwell, 1996).
6. "Esplanade Avenue," Official Tourism Site of the City of New Orleans, NewOrleansOnline. com (accessed October 23, 2012).

7. Michelle Krupa, "Blighted New Orleans Intersection at Broad, Washington Set for Transformation," *Times Picayune*, April 25, 2012.

8. Arnold Hirsch and Joseph Logsdon, "The People and the Culture," Department of History, University of New Orleans, NewOrleansOnline.com (accessed January 2013).

9. Lawton Evans, "De Soto Discovers the Mississippi," Baldwin Project, mainlesson.com (accessed March 2014).

10. Garvey and Widmer, *Beautiful Crescent*.

11. Ibid.

12. Evans, "De Soto Discovers the Mississippi."

13. Garvey and Widmer, *Beautiful Crescent*.

14. Robert Weddle, "Tonti, Henri de," Handbook of Texas Online, tshaonline.org/handbook (accessed May 14, 2014).

15. "Letter of Henry de Tonti, Left for La Salle with Indians in 1685," Hancock County Historical Society, http://www.hancockcountyhistoricalsociety.com (accessed March 2013).

16. Ibid.

17. Garvey and Widmer, *Beautiful Crescent*.

18. John Smith Kendall, *History of New Orleans* (Chicago and New York: Lewis Publishing Company, August 1922).

19. Garvey and Widmer, *Beautiful Crescent*.

20. Hirsch and Logsdon, "People and the Culture."

21. Sally Reeves, "Is the French Quarter French or Spanish?" New Orleans French Quarter History, frenchquarter.com (accessed March 2013).

22. Hirsch and Logsdon, "People and the Culture."

23. Sharon Keating, "A Short History of New Orleans," Go New Orleans, http://goneworleans.about.com (accessed February 2014).

Part II

24. Garvey and Widmer, *Beautiful Crescent*.

25. Lee Smith, "Women in Colonial Louisiana," *Encyclopedia of Louisiana*, Louisiana Endowment for the Humanities, May 21, 2011.

26. Emily Clark, "Masterless Mistresses: The New Orleans Ursulines and the Development of a New World Society, 1727–1834," Omohundro Institute of Early American History and Culture, Williamsburg, Virginia, 2007.

27. Yves Landry, *Orphelins en France, Pionières au Canada: Les Filles du Roi au XVIIE Siècle* (Montréal, CAN: Leméac, 1992).

28. Liz Smith, "The Casket Girls of New Orleans: Founding Matriachs or Vampire Smugglers," Go New Orleans, http://goneworleans.about.com (accessed August 2011).

29. Shirley Hodges, "Was Your Grandmother a Casket Girl?" Global Genealogy, July 2010, globalgenealogy.com (accessed February 2014).

30. Colleen Landry, "Ursuline Academy and Convent in New Orleans Before and After Katrina," October 2005, http://www.pbase.com/septembermorn/ursuline_academy_and_convent_after_hurricane_katrina (accessed February 2014).

31. Carter Woodson and Charles H. Wesley, *The Story of the Negro Retold* (Rockville, MD: Wildside Press, LLC, 2008)

32. Stacy Le Melle, "Quadroons for Beginners: Discussing the Suppressed and Sexualized History of Free Women of Color with Author Emily Clark," Huffington Post, September 2013, http://www.huffingtonpost.com/stacy-parker-aab/quadroons-for-beginners-d_b_3869605.html (accessed May 2014).

33. Ibid.

34. Ibid.

35. Ibid.

36. Elizabeth Wilson, "Sinning for Silk," Womens Studies International Forum, 1987.

37. Al Rose, *Storyville, New Orleans: Being an Authentic Illustrated Account of the Notorious Red-Light District* (Tuscaloosa: University of Alabama Press, 1974).

38. *Times Picayune*, "1903: Storyville, New Orleans' Red-Light District, Was Famous," October 2011, nola.com.

39. Wilson, "Sinning for Silk."

40. Rose, *Storyville, New Orleans*.

41. Wilson, "Sinning for Silk."

42. Nancy E. Rexford, *Women's Shoes in America, 1795–1930* (Kent, OH: Kent State University Press, 2000).

43. Ibid.

44. Lyle Saxon, *A Collection of Louisiana Folk Tales: Gumbo Ya-Ya* (Louisiana Writers' Project of the Work Projects, 1945; reprint, New York: Bonanza Books, 1984).

45. Wilson, "Sinning for Silk."

46. Mary P. Ryan, *Womanhood in America: From Colonial Times to the Present* (New York: Franklin Watts, 1979).

47. *(New Orleans) Mascot,* January 5, 1889.

48. Wilson, "Sinning for Silk."

49. Rose, *Storyville, New Orleans.*

50. Ibid.

51. Alan Lomax, *Mister Jelly Roll: The Fortunes of Jelly Roll Morton, New Orleans Creole and Inventor of Jazz* (New York: Grosset & Dunlap, 1950).

52. Rose, *Storyville, New Orleans.*

53. Ibid.

54. Ibid.

55. *Times Picayne,* "1897 Maison Blanche Department Store Grand Opening," October 1, 2011, http://www.nola.com/175years/index.ssf/2011/10/1897_maison_blanche_department.html.

56. Ibid.

57. Jillian LaRochelle, "Like Father, Like Daughter" MRKETPLACE: Connecting the People, Ideas and Energy of the Menswear Business January 13, 2012. http://www.mrketplace.com/35660/like-father-like-daughter/ (accessed June 2014).

58. Missy Wilkinson, "Yvonne LaFleur," *Gambit Weekly,* July 19, 2011.

59. Al Rose and Edmond Souchon, *New Orleans Jazz: A Family Album* (Baton Rouge: Louisiana State University Press, 1978).

60. Kathleen Pondurant, "Survey of Music History, Roots of Jazz," PhD presentation, October 23, 2009, http://www.slideshare.net/DrBondurant/4-a-roots-of-jazz.

61. Samuel Charters, *Trumpet Around the Corner: The Story of New Orleans Jazz,* American Made Music Series (Oxford: University Press of Mississippi, 2008).

62. Ted Gioia, *The History of Jazz* (New York: Oxford University Press, 1997).

63. "Two Films Unveil a Lost Jazz Legend," National Public Radio, December 15, 2007, http://www.nps.gov/jazz/historyculture/bolden.htm.

64. Margaret Pick, "Mr. Jelly Lord: A Tribute to Jelly Roll Morton and His Red Hot Peppers," Riverwalk Jazz, 1992, http://riverwalkjazz.stanford.edu (accessed February 2014).

65. Ibid.

66. Ibid.

67. Scott Alexander, "Louis Armstrong," A History of Jazz Before 1930, Red Hot Jazz Archive, http://www.redhotjazz.com/louie.html (accessed February 2014).

68. Scott Alexander, "Duke Ellington," A History of Jazz Before 1930, Red Hot Jazz Archive http://www.redhotjazz.com/duke.html (accessed February 2014).

69. http://civilclothing.com/fashion-and-jazz/ (accessed May 2014).

70. "Biography Wynton Marsalis," Wynton Marsalis Enterprises, http://wyntonmarsalis.org/about/bio (accessed May 2014).

71. *Faubourg Tremé: The Untold Story of Black New Orleans*, directed by Dawn Logsdon and Lolis Eric Elie (Berkeley, CA: Serendipity Films, LLC, 2008).

72. Missy Wilkinson, "New Orleans Fashion Profiled in a New Oxford American Column," *Gambit Weekly*, March 27, 2012.

73. Ibid.

74. Jack Stewart, *Funerals with Music in New Orleans* (New Orleans, LA: Save Our Cemeteries, Incorporated, and J. Stewart, 2004).

75. Richard Brent Turner, *Jazz, Religion, the Second Line, and Black New Orleans* (Bloomington: Indiana University Press, 2009).

76. Matt Sakakeeny, "Jazz Funerals and Second Line Parades," KnowLA Encyclopedia of Louisiana, March 25, 2012.

77. Karol Nolan, *Vintage Fashions* (New York: Harper, 1968).

78. Jackie Hatton, "Flappers," *St. James Encyclopedia of Popular Culture* (Detroit, MI: St. James Press, 2000).

79. Nicholas Hennell-Foley, "The Influence of Jazz on Women's Fashion and Society in the 1920's," Academia. http://www.academia.edu/5034145/The_Influence_of_Jazz_on_Womens_Fashion_and_Society_in_the_1920s edu (accessed February 2014).

80. Ibid.

81. Ibid.

82. Henri Schindler, *Mardi Gras Treasures: Jewelry of the Golden Age* (Gretna, LA: Pelican Publishing Company, Inc., 2006).

83. Ibid.

84. Ibid.

85. Marc Antoine Caillot, "A Company Man: The Remarkable French-Atlantic Voyage of a Clerk for the Company of the Indies," Historic New Orleans Collection, New Orleans, 2013.

86. Schindler, *Mardi Gras Treasures*.

87. Arthur Hardy, "History of Mardi Gras," New Orleans Online http://www.neworleansonline.com/neworleans/mardigras/ (accessed February 2014).

88. Cynthia Becker, "New Orleans Mardi Gras Indians: Mediating Racial Politics from the Backstreets to Main Street," *African Arts* (June 2013).

89. Ibid.

90. Susan Tselos, "Threads of Reflection: Costumes of Haitain Rara," *African Arts* (1996).

91. Becker, "New Orleans Mardi Gras Indians."

92. Gail Pellett, "Mardi Gras Indians: Larry Bannock" *PBS Newshour*, 1984.

93. Ibid.

94. Kim Vaz, *The Baby Dolls: Breaking the Race and Gender Barriers of the New Orleans Mardi Gras Tradition* (Baton Rouge: LSU Press, 2013).

95. Tina Antolini, "The 'Baby Dolls' of Mardi Gras: A Fun Tradition with a Serious Side," NPR, February 16, 2013.

96. Schindler, *Mardi Gras Treasures*.

97. Ibid.

98. Ibid.

99. Ibid.

100. Judy Walker, "Julia Reed's Book Showcases Her Usual Sparkle," *Times Picayune*, May 9, 2013.

101. Missy Wilkinson, "Yvonne LaFleur" *Gambit Weekly*, July 19, 2011.

102. Florence Hartley, *The Ladies' Book of Etiquette, and Manual of Politeness* (New York: G. Blackie & Co., 1826).

103. Jessica Baker, "The Coco Chanel Rules to Live By," *Who What Wear*, August 9, 2013, http://www.whowhatwear.com/the-coco-chanel-style-rules-to-live-by/ (accessed June 2014).

104. Brandon Dyce, "Where Pants Should Break," AskMen: Become a Better Man, March 2013 http://uk.askmen.com/fashion/fashiontip_300/317b_fashion_advice.html (accessed May 2014).

105. Jolie Bensen, "Seersucker," Jolie & Elizabeth, http://www.jolieandelizabeth.com/#!seersucker/c1yrr accessed (March 2014).

106. *New York Times*, "Men's Style: Puckering Up," May 22, 1988, http://www.nytimes.com/1988/05/22/magazine/men-s-style-puckering-up.html.

107. Ibid.

108. David Colman, "Summer Cool of Different Stripe," *New York Times*, April 20, 2006.

109. Ibid.

110. Stephen Yafa, *Cotton: The Biography of a Revolutionary Fiber* (New York: Penguin, 2006).

111. Jolie Bensen, "The Economic Oversight in Manufacturing Cotton (Part 2)," Huffington Post, February, 5, 2013, http://www.huffingtonpost.com/jolie-bensen/the-economic-oversight-manufacturing2_b_2573840.html (accessed May 2014).

Part III

112. "Uptown," NewOrleansOnline.com, http://www.neworleansonline.com/tools/neighborhoodguide/uptown.html (accessed February 2014).

113. "Carrollton/Riverbend Neighborhood," https://www.facebook.com/Carrollton.Riverbend/info (accessed February 2014).

114. "Uptown," NewOrleansOnline.com.

115. Ibid.

116. Shern Sharma and Melena Ryzik, "The Fashionable French Quarter," *New York Times*, January 28, 2014, video: http://www.nytimes.com/video/fashion/100000002674203/french-quarter-new-orleans-fashion-intersection.html?playlistId=100000001775830.

117. *Faubourg Tremé*.

118. Ibid.

119. Ibid.

120. Rick Jervis, "New Orleans Neighborhood Boasts Rich History," *USA Today*, February 21, 2012.

121. Ibid.

122. Chris Turner-Neal, "Red Beans and Tambourines: Kermit's Tremé Speakeasy Restaurant." GoNOLA.com February 22, 2013, http://www.gonola.com/2013/02/22/red-beans-and-tambourines-kermits-treme-speakeasy-restaurant.html.

123. Sarah Hudson, "NOLA Neighborhood Top 10: Tremé," GoNOLA.com, January 20, 2014, http://www.gonola.com/2014/01/20/nola-neighborhood-top-10-treme.html.

124. Sarah Costello, "Travel Diary|The Intoxicating, Tradition-Steeped Charm of New Orleans," *New York Times*, October 3, 2013, http://tmagazine.blogs.nytimes.com/2013/10/03/travel-diary-the-intoxicating-tradition-steeped-charm-of-new-orleans/?_php=true&_type=blogs&_r=0 (accessed February 2014).

125. "Fauboug Marigny and Bywater," NewOrleansOnline.com, http://www.neworleansonline.com/tools/neighborhoodguide/marigny.html (accessed February 2014).

126. Kat Krader, "Kat Krader's Insiders Guide to New Orleans," *Food and Wine Magazine* (November 2012).

127. Costello, "Travel Diary | The Intoxicating, Tradition-Steeped Charm of New Orleans."

128. "America's Most Visited City Parks," The Trust for Public Land, archived from the original on July 25, 2006, tpl.org (accessed February 2014).

129. "Arts District (Warehouse District)," NewOrleansOnline.com, http://www.neworleansonline.com/tools/neighborhoodguide/artsdistrict.html (accessed February 2014).

INDEX

ABOUT THE AUTHOR

Andi Eaton, named one of the most stylish people in the South by *Southern Living* magazine, is the designer of Hazel & Florange, a women's wear clothing line and celebration of southern charm inspired by the city of New Orleans. Her blog, Oui We, chronicles her personal style, travels and the stories of the Louisiana fashion community. She's the founder of the Southern Coalition of Fashion and Design, an organization dedicated to building a resource network for independent southern designers and those working in connected industries.

She's the founder of NOLA Fashion Week, which over three years has produced more than one hundred events and shows giving designers a platform to show their clothing to editors, buyers and trendsetters and also provides an educational program and a market place.